T·A·K·E C·O·N·T·R·O·

DRUG ABUSI
the facts about today's c

Books supplying expert information and practical guidance to help YOU take control

Titles published so far include

ALCOHOLISM
an insight into the addictive mind
Dr Clive Graymore

•

STROKE!
a self help manual for relatives and carers
Dr R. M. Youngson

•

SCHIZOPHRENIA
a fresh approach
Gwen Howe

•

FERTILITY
a comprehensive guide to natural family planning
Dr Elizabeth Clubb and Jane Knight

•

HEALTH DEFENCE
strengthen your immune defence system
Dr Caroline Shreeve

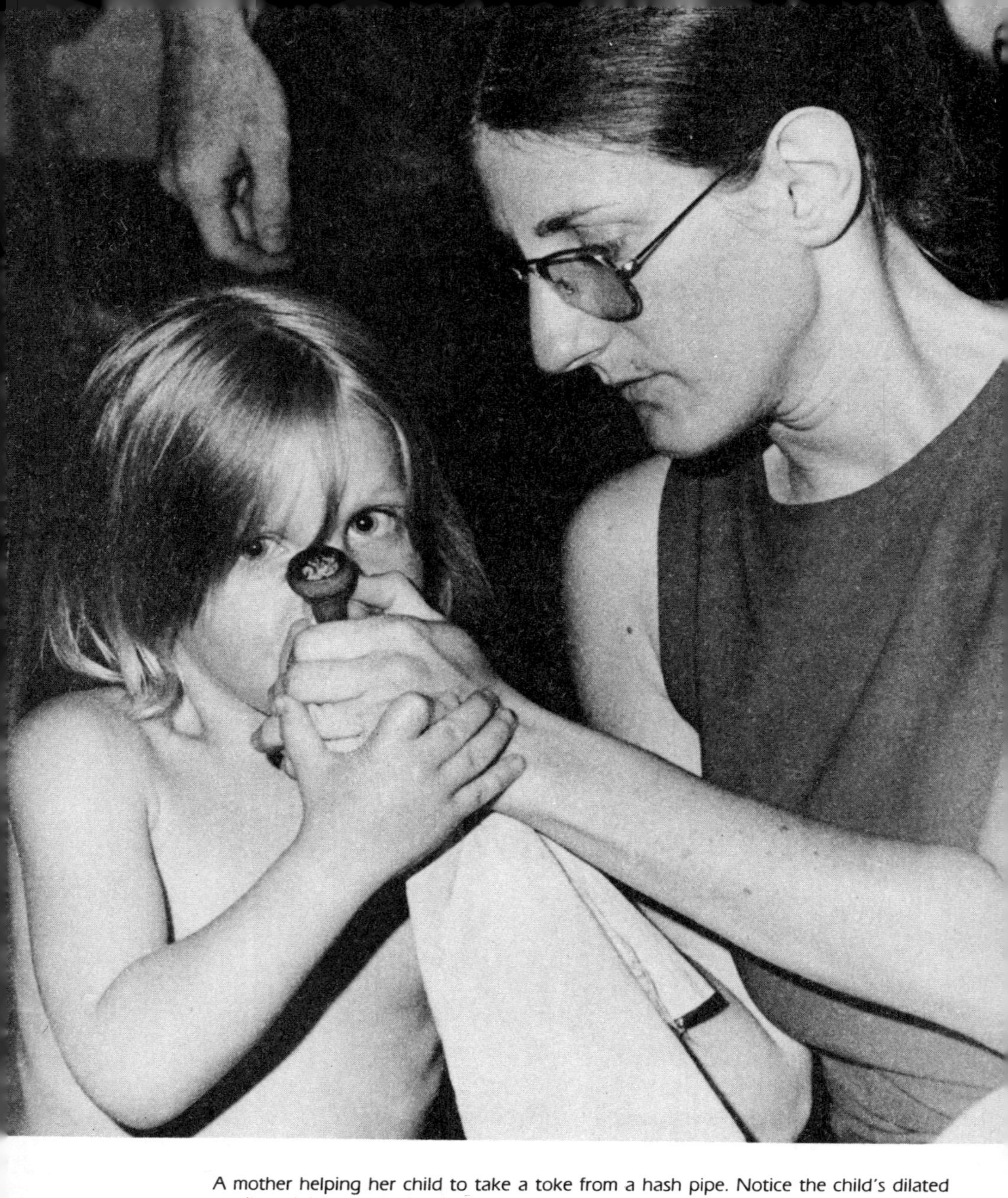

A mother helping her child to take a toke from a hash pipe. Notice the child's dilated pupils and the way she is gripping onto her mother's hand to prevent her taking the pipe away.
(*Topham*)

DRUG ABUSE

the facts about today's drug scene

Tony Blaze-Gosden

A DAVID & CHARLES health book

In Memory of
Edward and May Gosden
of
Edinburgh

British Library Cataloguing in Publication Data

Gosden, Tony Blaze
Drug abuse: the facts about today's
drug scene. – (Take control)
1. Drug abuse
I. Title II. Series
362.2'93 HV5081

ISBN 0-7153-9038-4

Typeset by Typesetters (Birmingham) Ltd,
Smethwick, West Midlands
and printed in Great Britain
by Billing and Sons Limited, Worcester
for David & Charles Publishers plc
Brunel House Newton Abbot Devon

Contents

Foreword

Parents and relatives are fed up with being hectored and lectured by politicians, social workers, and do-gooders about their alleged inadequacies in respect of their children.

My aim is to give families the chance to stand as equals amongst the so-called experts. To give them the ammunition with which they can put these people into their correct perspective. To enable them to restore their badly eroded rights and status as parents and deal with the 'experts' secure in their *own* knowledge and understanding of the subject of drug abuse. To put the family centre stage in the war against drugs in defence of their young people against the drug dealers. It is best that young peoples' knowledge of the true dangers of drug abuse comes from within a caring and well-informed family. This book is written for anyone anywhere who wants to take part in the war against drugs.

Much in this book is based on my personal experience of drug addicts, drug dealers, manufacturers, and traffickers over a period of forty years. My first observations of the destructive effects of the drug trade and drug addiction were made when I was a young sailor in the West Indies and Americas Squadron of the Royal Navy, shortly after the Second World War. Later, as an Officer in the Royal Hong Kong Police Force, I commanded drug squads on land and by sea.

In the course of my police career I was able to see, at first hand, how the spread of drug addiction infiltrated, corrupted, and poisoned the whole of society. Despite the strenuous efforts of honest police and customs officers, drugs constantly poured in by sea and air, and made their best seizures seem like molehills in contrast to the mountains of heroin and opium that got through. The law-enforcers were few, but the drug barons had legions of helpers paid for out of the millions of pounds of drug profits. By the time I was forced to retire, as a result of a mounting tally of wounds and injuries, the drug traffickers were using modern technology to further their trade. This includes sophisticated communications equipment, air flights from the Golden Triangle with drugs dropped by parachute to waiting boats off the coast, fast boats, an efficient distribution system, and skilled financial experts to spirit the profits away. The police and customs in the United Kingdom are now facing the same problems. Every addict and drug dealer is a member of the drug barons' army and, together with those who work just for the money, they outnumber all the drug squads in the United Kingdom by thousands to one! Drug squad duty is a rotten, dangerous job. The injuries inflicted on the officers in the course of their duty are easily dealt with and are accepted as part of the job, but the injuries which may be inflicted on an officer's career by false allegations of brutality or corruption are not so easily remedied, and some politicians, senior officers, and the media seem more eager to believe lying addicts than the officers. Despite this members of the drug squads carry on and serve the public well, within the constraints imposed upon them.

Apart from large and well-publicised seizures of drugs, the public have little knowledge of how and why drug addiction is spreading visibly in Britain. Much of the information we receive is distorted by the media, in films, or in the statements of politicians and interest groups. People want to know what is really happening, why it is happening, and what is being done about it.

The answers to the questions raised are contained in this book, together with some suggestions of possible future action to curb the drug traffic. There are, in my opinion, no 'soft drugs' and 'hard drugs'. All of the drugs being traded to addicts and users are dangerous drugs, and I do not, therefore, offer any soft options. Incidentally, I have used 'he' and 'him' throughout the book as a matter of convenience, but there are, in fact, almost as many female addicts as male.

It is my hope that the contents of this book will serve to inform the ordinary, concerned, man and woman, and give them not only details about the drugs and their use but also some background information – as ammunition in the war of words – about what should be done to stop the plague of drug addiction.

Tony Blaze-Gosden
South Wales

PART I
Addiction

1 Why the fuss?

Worried parents and other members of society generally are very concerned by the obvious spread of illegal drugs throughout the country; and the threat posed to children, communities, and the nation. They want to know what it is all about, but usually find that, either the language being used is unintelligible to them, or the information does not tally with what they hear from friends and neighbours, or it sounds like sociological jargon.

Even a visit to the local library may not help, as many of the books and articles dealing with drug abuse are so academic or technical that they are almost impossible for ordinary folk to decipher.

Officialdom may also fail them, as some officials and departments are so determined to avoid controversial horror stories, that they go to the other extreme and neglect to make the point that drug addiction ruins lives. Some of the leaflets which are issued on drug abuse take this low-key approach to the extent that addiction seems almost harmless, or at least not much worse than a dose of influenza.

This book is written for people who know little or nothing about drugs, drug abuse, drug dealing, or the drug traffic generally, but want to find out. It is for everyone who doesn't know where to seek information, or is unable to obtain the information in an understandable form, or is too shy or too embarrassed to ask about it.

Almost invariably the first question asked of anyone who is involved in any anti-drugs activity, or who is giving drugs talks, is 'Who becomes a drug addict' and there is almost universal disbelief, sometimes annoyance, at the reply 'Your kid'. The answer is not strictly accurate, for there is no age discrimination in drug addiction. In fact, anyone may become addicted to any one of the 28 commonest drugs of addiction, or to any combination of them. However, the most favoured targets of the drug merchants are young people, for the simple reason that they are more easily tricked into trying out, or experimenting, with drugs and, by virtue of their youth, they are more able to cheat, steal, and ultimately to sell their bodies in prostitution, in order to pay for the drugs they will then need, and have to obtain, just in order to function.

Drugs are a world-wide problem, and the information in this book is relevant to every country in the world. Traditionally, for people who have lived most of their lives in countries such as the United Kingdom, drug addiction has been something seen in the cinema, or on television, or read about in novels, in locations like Chinatown, New York, and the characters have been orientals or Italian Americans. It is only now that the reality is becoming apparent, that drug addicts include the nice boy or girl next door or, even worse, the nice children who should be upstairs in bed. The British or New Zealanders, for example, have had no background knowledge or understanding of the drug traffic, which is more of an intrinsic part of growing up for some children in parts of America, Hong Kong, or Japan.

There is no identikit psychological or physical profile of a typical addict. Drug addiction is like some biblical plague that can strike high and low, rich and poor, beautiful and ugly, young and old, yet it is the young who are most at risk, especially those in their teens, or sub-teens. This is the time when most youngsters are at the period of change. They are moving away from general acceptance of parental and elder control and values, and are just beginning to assert their own individuality.

This assertion of individuality is usually accompanied by what seems, to puzzled parents, to be an almost sheeplike but determined desire to look, and behave, like every other youngster in their age group, from their choice of clothes, hair styles and make up, to listening with glazed eyes to the same music and mooning over pop idols. For some, this assertion of individuality may include experimentation with drugs.

Politicians and policemen, doctors and social workers all have personal and professional opinions of the motives which cause people to become dependent on drugs, and it can hardly be surprising if political and professional bias colours their opinions to some extent. Politicians in the parties in opposition to the government in power put the blame firmly on the policies of the governing party, especially those policies which they claim cause unemployment, bad housing, and poverty – conditions which are always contrasted critically with an elite which, allegedly, enjoys luxury and riches. If this was entirely so, then there would be no evidence of drug abuse within the elite, yet the press and other media are constantly publicising the downfall, disgrace and even death of individuals who are members of the richest and most privileged classes in the country. This makes the ordinary man in the street wonder if all the experts know what they are talking about, and makes him mistrust their pronouncements.

Social workers, members of the 'caring' professions, some doctors and some politicians seem to put forward arguments which absolve the drug addicts from any personal responsibility for their condition, and implicitly blame external forces, such as the government, environmental or social factors. Most policemen are seen as holding cynical and biased views of both the cause of drug addiction and the drug addicts themselves.

In fact, in my experience, many policemen do not accept the 'apologies' put forward for the drug addicts, because of their personal experience of dealing with them. They think that, just as some people 'decide' to become criminals because that is their nature, so some people simply choose to become drug addicts because of a whim, because it is considered an anti-social habit, or to copy the manners, morals, and habits of their pop idols.

There is a middle ground, which contains elements of both the environmental and personal-choice arguments, but it may be overlooked by the opposing groups when they defend their personal and professional stances, as is the idea that some people possess an innate propensity to overindulge in drugs, just as others overindulge in food or alcohol. Many opposed views are honestly and sincerely held on the basis of published reports, papers and statistics, yet many of the statistics may not give an image that can be applied generally. The conclusions they draw may be based on data which is not strictly accurate. Most statistics are based on studies made in publicly funded or charitable institutions. In these types of institutions, a drug addict is listed as such, whereas wealthy and middle class addicts are, mainly, treated for their addiction privately and they may not appear in any public survey of drug abuse.

One of the hidden sectors of the medical profession is the

treatment of private patients for drugs and alcohol abuse, at fees which can exceed £3,000 per week. At this price, drug addiction may transform itself into a psychiatric condition which does not carry any stigma.

This does not imply any deceit on the part of the medical practitioners; after all, it may indeed be the underlying psychiatric condition that is being treated and not the drug addiction which is assumed to have occurred as a result of it. It is, however, because of this that a worried or anxious parent may take false hope and see no risk to a loved one, who is in danger, but does not fit into the generally accepted categories of people at risk. Anyone may become a drug addict even if, statistically, some people are more likely to do so than others. When considering stereotypes and statistics it must be kept in mind that they are only accurate and relevant when viewed within the framework of how they were gathered, and under what constraints and circumstances.

For example if, as suggested above, figures are collected from governmental or voluntary agencies, to which advanced drug addicts have been referred by hospitals, doctors, etc, or to which addicts have gone voluntarily, then any conclusions drawn from these figures must be seen as relating to advanced drug addicts in trouble, and must not be taken as being representative of those addicts who are currently satisfied with the level of their habit. A further exercise of care is very necessary when interviewing drug addicts or dealing with them in any way, as they have a great propensity for deceit. It is a fact that many drug addicts (and criminals) are very well versed in the jargon of sociology and psychiatry, and are ready to give the answers which they believe the questioner wants to hear. This is quite apart from a natural human tendency to blame someone or something else for their condition. This is especially so if the addict is recovering in decent accommodation, with regular meals, perhaps receiving some medically prescribed drug to ease his condition, and with no disciplinary controls such as would be imposed in prison. Such a stay in a treatment centre can seem like a holiday to an addict, until he feels fit enough to go back onto the streets, and to his habit. By its very nature, drug abuse is a secretive thing shared only by a brotherhood of addicts and dealers, who are almost instantly identifiable to each other by the secret marks of their habits, which would not be apparent to the ordinary non-addict. Drug addicts can lie as naturally as drawing breath, so assumptions must be made about drug addiction from *all* the evidence and information available. None of the data is absolutely accurate because drug traffickers and drug addicts do not provide statistics or accounts.

It was originally thought that the age groups which might be most at risk were those in the early twenties. It is now generally accepted that this is in fact the age at which long term addiction may become apparent. The groups most at risk of introduction to drug abuse are from 12 to about 16 years of age. Too young to overtly join their older friends in pub, club, or disco, but not too young to obtain drugs from a dealer. How this comes about is fairly similar everywhere.

The commonest scenario lies in the passive acceptance by parents of modern teenage pop-culture. Young people are permitted, even encouraged, to seek all of their social life and entertainment with their peer groups, without any adult supervision or control. Big business promotes the pop-culture for reasons of profit, and parents are almost brainwashed into accepting their children's rights – without any mention of children's obligations, or of exposure to moral and physical danger.

Truly caring parents, especially those in the racial minorities, are portrayed critically in the media for attempting to impose old-fashioned and uncivilized restrictions upon the social development of their children. Absolute self-determination is supposed to be the right of every child, no matter how immature. Some teachers and social workers encourage this attitude to an alarming degree, but they do not have to suffer the awful consequences. It is the parents who have to do so, usually in the face of criticism implying that it is their fault if a child has become addicted. Yet, with very few exceptions, it is during unsupervised activities with their friends that children and young people are at risk. This is especially so when they are allowed to get into an uncontrolled cycle of continuous or semi-continuous activities. Discos, parties or pop shows which always go on until the late hours, which happen night after night, followed by school or work and a fog of fatigue.

Inevitably, there comes the offer of the pill that will give a harmless lift to flagging energy, so that the user may enjoy the next round of fun; or the pill that will help with its calming effect if the pace is getting too hot; or the cannabis cigarette that will provide relief, relaxation, easing of inhibitions and mild euphoria. From these apparently helpful and harmless beginnings, starts the trail that may lead to a lifetime, for some a tragically short lifetime, of misery and addiction.

Danger may lurk at school, too, especially in the huge education mills created by politicians and teachers' unions in the 1960s. In the crowded and impersonal surroundings of the large city schools, the average individual students can become blurred educational statistics to the teaching staff, only coming to direct notice because of peculiarities of excellence or inferiority. In such surroundings, unsuitable friendships and liaisons can be established, and opportunities for the entrapment of the vulnerable can be exploited. Other pupils, on the lookout for drug customers to subsidise their own habit, or just looking to make money, can take full advantage of their anonymity in the crowd to ensnare the naive, the lonely, and those under stress. Even a pill, offered to relieve the strain and stress of examinations or hard study, can be enough for a start on the long slippery slope. The first one may be free, but for the rest it will be cash in advance.

The home can also be a place of risk. We have become a pill-popping society so accustomed to taking pills, for every physical and psychological discomfort, that we sometimes fail to recognise the danger of taking drugs other than under medical supervision. Babies only have to squeak and a pill is pushed into their mouths. In, on and around medicine cabinets, dressing tables and bedside tables in every country, there are possibly millions of sleeping pills, slimming pills, anti-depressant pills and tranquillisers, all legally obtained by means of a doctor's prescription. Parents and elders are seen taking these pills, as a matter of course, day after day. It is hardly surprising that young people follow the example set them by their elders, for the wrong reasons.

Drugs are available anywhere. From east to west and from north to south, the dealers and sub dealers and addicts with 'spare' are ready, willing and able to sell drugs of all types, at all times and in all places. Discos, pubs, clubs, fairgrounds, holiday resorts, housing estates, in and near schools, inner city high schools or comprehensives and prestigious boarding schools are all suitable places. Some of the dealers have regular pitches where addicts know they can contact them, or 'score', at any time. Addicts can arrive in a strange town and make a purchase within an hour or so, because they know the type of area haunted by their fellow addicts. They find and make contact with an obvious user, possibly posted there for that purpose, who will then direct them to the local dealer, usually for a small reward. The chain of supply from the drug baron to the local dealer is long, but well organised.

The product delivered to the buyer, in exchange for money, is a drug of abuse and addiction. The terms a 'hard' drug or 'soft' drug are nonsensical and very dangerous. It may be that there is an intention to discriminate between those drugs which are agreed to have a high potential for addiction, and those which are alleged to be less addictive. Whatever the reason, this false discrimination should stop. All drugs which cause a user to become a drug addict, other than those given under medical supervision, are dangerous to the user and to society.

It is possible that the so called 'soft' drug, herbal cannabis, is the most dangerous of all, as young people are being misled and confused by the incessant assertions by pop idols and some politicians (who should know better), that marijuana is no more dangerous than alcoholic drink. Cannabis is decidedly more dangerous, for a number of reasons, which are dealt with in detail later in this book. Principally it is more dangerous because the psychoactive, mind affecting, element in cannabis, the substance called THC has increased in power more than fifty fold since the 1960s. A similar increase in alcoholic potency would make a normal 30 tot bottle of rum serve the equivalent of 1,650 drinks in comparative potent effect. Alcohol is normally flushed out of the body within 24hr, but THC can remain in the body for a week or longer. It is also implicated in long term genetic effects upon users. Male sexual potency and sperm production are reduced. Similar reproductive potential is also reduced in the female, but the most serious worry is the genetic defects caused in babies. Almost everyone has heard of babies, born to addicted mothers, having withdrawal symptoms. There is nothing more heartrending than a beautiful baby twitching in spasms from a damaged nervous system that has resulted from its mother's drug abuse during pregnancy. We are familiar with thalidomide, but the horrors of drug abuse can produce much more disastrous results. There are no 'soft' drugs!

Almost everyone has heard something about illicit drugs, their abuse, addicts and the trafficking. Yet most ordinary people have scant or confused ideas about drug abuse, other than the sensationalised versions presented by the media, in fiction, or the confusing reports in academic, medical, legal or sociological works. Because of this lack of general knowledge, many ordinary folk despair of seeing any way of combating the menace. They simply fear for their families and their society, and some regard the present plague of drug abuse almost in the way that people in medieval Europe regarded the Black Death.

The object of this book is to give, in a compact and easily readable form, sufficient information for the ordinary reader to understand what are the main drugs of abuse; how they are grown and manufactured; how they are transported and sold; what addiction is and its long term effects; what help is available to the addict and to the family; and what remedies might be applied locally, nationally and internationally to suppress the drug trade.

2 Answers to basic questions

Definitions are the dry dust of reality. The addict's whole being is permeated, throughout all his waking hours, with the overwhelming need for the possession of his drug so that he may survive the terrifying period which must elapse until he gets his next supply. Life is a frenetic cycle of panic revolving around the necessity to have money to obtain the drug, to take it for a brief moment of comparative peace, before beginning again the frantic search for the means to find the money to buy more drugs. It must be understood, that this is not just a whim, or a strong desire; this is a craving stronger even than the wish to live. Every addict knows that every time he takes the drug he may die. Even if he suspects it may be diluted with strychnine, DDT powder, scouring powder, or caustic, he must have his fix!

WHAT IS A 'DRUG'?

In this book 'drug' means any chemical or plant-derived substance which can cause any person using it to experience mental, emotional, or physical change, and the use of which for these purposes is illegal.

WHAT IS A DRUG ADDICT AND A DRUG USER?

An addict is any person who habitually takes any chemical or plant-derived substance – other than food, and for other than medical reasons – in order to obtain a desired mental, emotional, or physical effect, or to satisfy a craving, and who is dependent on this substance; or simply any person addicted to a habit-forming drug. A drug user is any person who consumes drugs, whether addicted or not.

WHO BECOMES A DRUG ADDICT?

Anybody may become a drug addict, whether a resident of some sprawling housing estate or of a ducal palace.

WHY DO PEOPLE BECOME DRUG ADDICTS?

Many people have become addicted to slimming tablets, stimulants and tranquilizers through being given them in medical treatment. This was more common ten or twenty years ago, before the medical profession became aware of the danger of over-prescribing drugs to help people to relax, or sleep, or cope, lose weight, pep up, or ease down.

More recently, certainly over the last three decades, drugs seem to have achieved a glamour because the media, films, and popular music have all combined to show and publicise many of the glamorous people – film stars, pop idols, the rich, the famous, and the important – all taking drugs as part of titillatingly interesting and exciting activities, far-removed from the realities of a dull job, or of unemployment, or of suburban life. Many of the most popular Sunday newspapers would be hard pressed for stories without the highly paid confessions of pop singers, film stars, their wives, partners or former friends.

This kind of media excess is not seen by the young as a warning to avoid the dangers of drug abuse; indeed, it is all presented in such a manner that youngsters can't be blamed for seeing the excitement, glamour and harmlessness of the 'hippy culture' but not the implicit dangers, and the folly of 'just trying drugs once'.

ARE ANY YOUNG PEOPLE PARTICULARLY AT RISK OF BECOMING ADDICTED?

A number of factors are most commonly quoted as cropping up in the background of many young addicts, but they are only possible factors, not definite causes. They include:

- A parent or parents who drink alcohol heavily
- Being brought up by a single parent for a significant period before the age of 16
- Being brought up in a family where the parents are constantly engaged in serious disagreements
- Being brought up in an institution
- Being the child of manual, or of unskilled, or of deprived parents; living on a council estate; being a member of a large family; having a conviction for some crime or offence whilst a juvenile
- Leaving home at an early age without employment or without alternative accommodation
- Living at home with a family, where one or more family members is an addict.

It must be borne in mind, however, that some of the most recently publicised drug scandals and tragedies have involved children of some of the most important people in Britain, and others who are the products of some of Britain's most highly regarded public schools and universities. They would hardly fit many of the factors given above.

It is necessary, therefore, to consider the more deeply rooted factors that play a part in causing young people of all backgrounds to turn to this evil as a diversion:

- Young people growing up feeling lonely, who lack parental care, companionship and friendship
- The destruction of the extended family with its closeness and provision of alternative familial support and guidance when parents and offspring cannot communicate
- Youngsters growing up without adequate supervision and discipline
- An abandonment of old virtues and certainties, with no new or alternative replacements of value
- Youngsters receiving little or no moral or religious teaching to fall back on. The failure of many religious institutions in their traditional religious work
- Active encouragement by the media and pop culture for young people to be cynical; to have hatred of any authority, discipline, or parental control; the erosion, by mockery, of self respect
- A general harping on the topic of personal rights but practically nothing said about personal responsibilities.

WHAT AGE GROUP IS MOST AT RISK?

This may vary around the country, but it seems, from some evidence, that 12 to 16 years of age is the most dangerous period, followed by the 16 to 20 age group.

WHY DO PEOPLE USE DRUGS?

This is the $64,000 question. If the answer to this question could be clearly established, then drug abuse could easily be prevented. However, there are some clues.

Because of the glamorisation of drug abuse, the constant headlines and publicity accorded to anything and anyone connected with drugs, the young are drawn to experiment with drugs. The dangers and high risks attached to them are well publicised but even the fact that their parents are generally against drugs, all add to the lure. Curiosity about them, showing off, wanting to be one of the gang, all these factors may contribute. For youngsters who are unsure of themselves in adolescence – with emotional problems, with family problems, or school problems, or problems with their social life (or lack of it), with frustrations in general – any drug they may be tempted to try might give them the effects they need, at least in the early stages. Pleasant floating sensations, feelings of ease and comfort, or strength and vitality, exhilaration, relief of inhibitions, feelings of competence and capability, of being in charge of their fate – these are experienced in the early days of drug taking.

Even in the fog caused by hallucinogens like LSD, people may feel a superior sense of insight, vision, and experience denied to the common herd. All very attractive to a lumpy, spotty faced, insecure adolescent going through the trauma of the teens; of being too old to play kids' games, and too young to be accepted as adult by his or her family. As to the harmful effects, those who take the first step on the road to drug addiction usually take it believing of a surety that they will be like those other characters who can 'take it or leave it', who can 'stay in charge'. Sadly few do.

FROM WHOM DO THEY GET THEIR FIRST FIX?

Nearly three-quarters of all addicts were given their first drugs by a friend; only about one in ten received their first fix from a dealer. It should be borne in mind, though, that dealers actively encourage their customers to get their friends started on drugs and will frequently arrange special deals, at reduced prices, to hook more customers. So the statement that is frequently made, that dealers rarely start people on drugs, may be true on the surface but, in fact, dealers are still responsible since they are merely employing addicts as agents to do their dirty work of recruitment.

WHERE DO THEY USUALLY TAKE THEIR FIRST DOSE OF DRUGS?

It could be at school, college or university. Friends offer pep pills to 'keep them going' while studying after late nights. At a disco or pub, some youngsters want something extra, over and above alcohol, to overcome shyness and give them new courage and identity. At youth clubs they are offered euphorics added to alcohol to compensate for emotional and social problems. During any group activity that involves sport or physical activity some may take drugs to produce actual physical strength and stamina. Others take them just to be accepted by their peer groups. In fact anywhere, if activities are badly or negligently supervised, drugs may be found. It is in unsupervised group activities with their friends that young people are most at risk. Parents who are silly enough to allow their adolescent children to attend parties without some parental supervision are simply asking for disaster!

WHAT ARE THE DANGER SIGNS?

There are signs, which may become apparent if parents or teachers or youth leaders are aware of them and are alert to their possible significance. It must be remembered, though, that what might appear to be drug danger signals could turn out to be only the normal processes of adolescence, which all parents must suffer.

At home

- Money and easily sold goods, such as tape recorders and jewellery, start disappearing from the home
- Sons or daughters being absent from the home more than before, or ceasing to attend youth club, or dropping school activities, which were previously enjoyed
- Carelessness about appearance – wearing scruffy clothes and looking unkempt
- Unusual displays of temper, frequently with no apparent cause
- Lack of appetite; sometimes excused by claims of dieting
- Wearing sunglasses at unusual times, usually to hide the odd look of pupils enlarged or reduced by drugs
- Wearing long sleeved clothes at unusual times, for example, on hot sunny days or at the beach, usually to hide needle marks in the arms
- Excessive use of aftershave or perfume to hide the smell of drugs
- Unusual borrowing of money with no evidence of any purchases
- Consistent paleness of complexion; unusual state of fatigue or excitation; becoming droopy and languid, alternating with excessive high spirits or moroseness.

At the school or youth group

- Parents may be alerted by reports from teachers or youth leaders who have noticed changes in their child's behaviour whilst supervising their activities
- Being the subject of gossip by other children indicating that they are taking drugs
- Keeping apart from other pupils or youth club members, and remaining away from their natural gathering points
- Being suspected of involvement in organised thefts
- Associating with an older person who is not a normal member of the youngster's usual group
- Dropping a friend for no reason
- Unusual absences from school or from appropriate activities in the school or youth group
- Using slang used by addicts (see drugs list).

IS DRUG ABUSE JUST A PROBLEM OF THE INNER CITIES?

Drug abuse is a problem everywhere especially where young people in groups are enjoying themselves. Dealers even have summer arrangements at summer camps or in holiday areas. In Britain, examples include Devon and Cornwall and Wales, and resorts such as Brighton and Blackpool. Places where young people congregate on holiday without parental supervision are easy targets. In such places it might be appropriate to exchange the picture postcards of the idyllic holiday scene for postcards of the village heroin seller.

WHAT CAN I DO IF I SUSPECT A MEMBER OF MY FAMILY IS TAKING DRUGS?

First, stay calm. Do not panic or explode into recriminations, or burst into tears. None of these courses of action is particularly useful. In any case, it must be remembered that much of the apparent evidence of drug taking is also characteristic of young people reaching that dreadful stage of puberty, with which most parents are only too familiar. At this stage young people's systems have increased their hormone production, and many seem to change, almost overnight, from well-loved children into scruffy, argumentative teenagers. They are not necessarily addicts, they are just being adolescent in the 1980s. So the first thing to do is take a deep breath, remember your own adolescence, and bear in mind the fact that, although drug abuse is increasing very rapidly, the majority of youngsters are not interested in taking drugs, only a minority.

If, however, you still believe that your child has started taking drugs, look for skilled, professional help. There are numerous organisations, services, voluntary self-help groups, agencies, etc from which you can receive help that is skilled, experienced, professional and sympathetic. Get in touch with them. You can find their addresses and phone numbers in libraries, schools, post offices, health centres, Citizens' Advice Bureau and doctor's surgeries.

Finally, do not feel personally guilty if your child has started taking drugs. It is not necessarily your fault. One of the most serious effects of drug addiction, especially where the addict has died, is the awful guilt felt by parents, who may feel that they have let their child down. Parents' rights over their children have been eroded for years by the media, by politicians, by bureaucrats and even by the courts. It is difficult for any parents to insist on basic behaviour and discipline from their children nowadays without being criticised as

Victorian throwbacks. If you have done your best against all the odds of external influences over your children, then you have no cause for guilt.

The addresses of some help agencies and organisations are given at the back of this book.

WHAT MAY BE THE LONG TERM EFFECTS ON THE FAMILY AND THE DRUG ADDICT IF TREATMENT IS REFUSED?

With the best will in the world any family can only take a certain amount of disruption caused by having a drug addict in the home. This includes theft, deceit and outrageous behaviour, including theft from relations, family, friends, neighbours, school friends and fellow pupils. Eventually everyone has had enough. Sympathy and toleration run out and the addict is quite understandably rejected by everyone he or she knows. The addict finds it easier to be with other drug takers and either moves out of the home or is thrown out by exasperated parents. There is then an almost inevitable involvement with the police. For both girls and boys there is the degradation of prostitution and stealing for the money needed to buy drugs. In addition to all the possible ill-effects and diseases caused by the drugs, there must be included the certainty of venereal disease and the high risk of contracting AIDS. This cycle of theft-prison-prostitution-arrest-prison-attempted cures is almost inevitable. Few addicts can find the minimum of $100 or £50 per day needed to fund a heroin habit (or even the $10 or £5 a day for a mild cannabis habit) without theft or prostitution. The only alternatives to giving up drugs are prison, disease, degradation and possible death.

ARTICLES AND OBJECTS THAT MAY INDICATE DRUG ABUSE

Drug users need paraphernalia of all kinds to take their drugs and all drugs come in some sort of container, even the pills. Parents should be alert for metal spoons discoloured by heat; small bottles; pill boxes; straws, usually cut quite short; spent matches; cigarette lighters; small pieces of tin foil discoloured by heat; twists of paper; small packets; butane gas containers; plastic bags, used in solvent abuse; tubes made of cardboard or any other materials, used to sniff heroin, cocaine etc; scraps of paper or plastic, about 2 inches square, folded like an envelope or sachet to hold heroin or other powdered drugs; pieces of paper, like stamps, which seem to have been in the mouth, for LSD dots; cigarette papers; pieces or shreds of tobacco and cannabis; syringes and needles.

These items are unlikely to be found lying around any youngster's room, but are usually secreted away under floorboards, under carpets, in the base of divan beds, garden sheds, garages or vacant houses, play dens, old outside toilets or anywhere that might seem a good hiding place and private.

DISEASES AND CONDITIONS PRESENTING PARTICULAR RISK TO DRUG USERS

Drug users who inject their drugs are the ones most at risk from a variety of diseases and ailments, ranging from minor infections at the point of injection to AIDS. Many of those who use the 'needle' increase their chances of dying by adding the danger factor of 'needle disease' to the danger factor of drug abuse. Dirty, unsterile syringes, needles and other equipment, and communal sharing, are the main sources of disease and infection. Because of this, it has been suggested that the free issue to addicts of disposable needles and syringes might reduce the risks of disease. The argument is that addicts would use the needles once only and then dispose of them carefully so as to cause no harm to other people such as dustbin men. This would be a good thing – if it worked – but it is to be wondered if the average needle-using addict would be clear-headed enough, or public-spirited enough, to remember to use a needle only once on himself, then carefully wrap it so as not to harm the dustbin men and then to dispose of it carefully in a dustbin so that no innocent person could be injured by it! It may not be unreasonable to think that the general nature and character of drug addicts does not give the impression that they are able to care for others, show public spiritedness or a social conscience, or indeed care for anything other than the drug of their addiction.

AIDS – Acquired Immune Deficiency Syndrome

AIDS is one of the newest diseases to threaten the populations of the western democracies, although it is believed to have existed in some African countries for some time. AIDS first came to public attention in western society when it hit the headlines as the homosexuals' disease in San Francisco and in New York, and when it later appeared in Canada and the UK.

The cause of the disease is believed to be a virus (HTLV111). The most serious effects of the disease are that the cells in the bloodstream which normally help to protect the body against disease become unable to combat a wide range of infectious diseases; in addition certain cancers may develop. AIDS victims are very sick people and many die of disease and cancers. Addicts who catch AIDS may pass it on to others by syringe, by sex, or by any other method by which blood or body fluids may transfer to another person's system.

Abscess

A collection of pus or 'matter' in some part of the body, usually just under the skin near the injection sites. If untreated, this may cause more serious conditions.

Anaemia

The reduction of the number of red corpuscles in the blood can cause various forms of anaemia. These corpuscles are the means by which oxygen from the air in the lungs is carried to all parts of the body. Oxygen is essential for the health of all living tissue. Victims of anaemia are usually pale, easily tired, may be short of breath, and commonly suffer from headaches. Women suffer more from anaemia than men as their monthly periods cause a drain on their red blood cells.

Anaesthesia

The state induced by a substance that abolishes physical pain. The substance is usually administered by injection or by inhaling a gas.

Asphyxia

Suffocation when the body is deprived of oxygen. It may occur in a number of ways; by obstructing the windpipe with vomit; by breathing gases which lack oxygen; by failure of the muscles that move the chest to draw air into the lungs; by drowning.

Blood pressure

The use of drugs may raise the blood pressure until the heart can no longer cope with the strain. This could result in a heart attack or a ruptured blood vessel in some important organ such as the brain.

Cellulitis

A spreading infection of the skin due to invasion by the streptococcus bacterium. In addicts this occurs usually at the site of the injections. The affected area becomes red, swollen and painful and needs expert treatment.

Coma

A state of unconsciousness produced by many different causes but quite commonly from drug abuse. The victim may choke if given anything by mouth.

Convulsion

Violent and abnormal muscular contraction of the body; spasms; fit. In some cases, drug-induced convulsions may cause serious injury or death.

Coronary infarction

Heart attack caused by a blood clot, by blockage of one of the small blood vessels leading to the heart. The clot may be introduced into the blood by drug injection.

Embolism

A clot of blood which is carried round the bloodstream until it lodges in a blood vessel and blocks it. This is always a serious condition.

Gangrene

A condition in which part of the body dies, usually due to interference with the circulation of blood which may be as a result of a blood clot in one of the vessels. Amputation is frequently the only possible treatment.

Hallucination

A condition in which something which does not really exist is perceived. Perception may be by any of the senses of sight, sound or touch.

Hepatitis

Inflammation of the liver caused by germs or virus which reach it from the bloodstream or the digestive tract.

Insomnia

Inability to sleep. Sleeplessness over a long period causes exhaustion and depression.

Jaundice

The liver makes bile which is stored in the gall bladder and pours from there into the intestine to aid in the digestion of fats. This function can be upset by germs or a virus, and if the bile cannot escape into the bowel it is forced back into the liver and enters the bloodstream. The tissues of the body and skin become coloured yellow by the bile.

Psychosis

Medical term for a condition of insanity.

THE FINAL OUTCOME

The end result for anyone who cannot give up drug addiction is a dreadful cycle of degradation, disease and death. This includes cheating, stealing and prostitution by boys and girls alike, followed by arrest, probation, arrest, imprisonment, arrest again, and so on.

Few addicts start off by injecting their drugs, but as they become more addicted they tend to begin injecting because they can get a bigger kick from smaller quantities of drugs, or from drugs that have been diluted until they are not powerful enough for smoking. They begin injecting in convenient veins in the arms. As they carry on injecting in the arms the veins collapse and they inject elsewhere. As fewer good veins are left, they progress to toes, to the arch of the feet and even to veins in the genitals; injections in the groin are particularly dangerous. Infections of all kinds are frequent, but the effects of the drug may hide the pain. Blood poisoning is common and, like the early symptoms of gangrene, may not be noticed until it is too late. There are hospital wards in the Far East and USA in which young teenagers have had amputations resulting from gangrene caused by needle tracks and there are mortuaries with the young dead waiting to be 'processed'.

All the claims for cures of drug addictions made so far relate to a very small number of people compared to the enormous rise in addiction. In any case a large number of the people cured slip back into the habit.

There used to be a public toilet by the Walled City in Kowloon, Hong Kong, which had a compound where the bodies of dead drug addicts were left for collection by the urban health department; they were then taken for disposal in rubbish trucks. That is the true reality of unchecked drug addiction, not soft words in gentle advertisements.

It is neither provocative nor alarmist to insist that the ultimate result for anyone who cannot give up drug abuse is degradation, disease, and death.

WHERE CAN AN ADDICT FIND ASSISTANCE TO GIVE UP DRUGS?

Help is available for any addict who wants to give up drugs.

There are self-help groups such as Narcanon, and there are also social and medical agencies. Addicts may get in touch with them through their doctors, social workers, probation officers, priests or ministers. A list of agencies is included at the end of this book but more addresses can be obtained from Post Offices, libraries, local papers, etc.

WHAT SHOULD I DO IF I SUSPECT SOME PLACE OR INDIVIDUAL IS INVOLVED IN DRUG DEALING?

Tell the police of your suspicious. You may go to a police station in person, or use the 'hotline' if you have one in your area. In the UK, you can write a letter to the chief constable of your county, or contact the Drugs Intelligence Unit in Scotland Yard, or inform your MP. In the US, you can contact your local law enforcement agency, or State Drug Abuse Prevention Coordinator, or your nearest DEA Division Office. If you are too frightened to identify yourself then make the call or send the letter anonymously. If the authorities get enough anonymous complaints about a person or place they must eventually investigate.

WHAT CAN I DO TO HELP STOP DRUG ABUSE?

- Inform your children and teach them about the horrors
- Encourage them to talk to other members of your family if they don't want to talk to you. Uncles, aunts, grandparents, cousins – everyone has a favourite member of the family
- Encourage schools and youth clubs to warn against drug abuse
- Form self-help information groups
- Join an organisation such as Parents Against Drug Abuse and put pressure on the government to do something to stamp out the drug trade
- If no anti-drugs organisation exists in your neighbourhood, start one!

PART II
Facts & Figures

3 Numbers and Costs

WORLDWIDE COST

The most recent figure for the annual cost to the world of drug abuse is US$300,000,000,000 – three hundred thousand million dollars – which is equal to, approximately, £207,000,000,000 – two hundred and seven thousand million pounds. This incredible amount of money goes into the private pockets of the drug barons for their personal benefit.

THE UNITED STATES

The USA, with its population of 242 million people, contributes about one third of this vast sum of money, about US$100,000,000,000 (£69 billion) through the purchases of its domestic drug users. The social costs and possible dangers to American society may be better understood by considering the extent and spread of drug abuse within the country. In 1985 it was estimated that over half a million Americans were addicted to heroin (although some estimates gave a figure of 1¼ million heroin addicts), 1 million were habitual users of hallucinogens, 20 million regularly used marijuana (cannabis), 6 million regularly abused prescription drugs, and between 8 million and 20 million used cocaine on a regular basis. This represents a total of 35½ million to 47½ million American drug abusers. At any given time between 1 in 7 (15%) and 1 in 5 (20%) of all American citizens may be going about their business or employment whilst under the effects of one or more drugs of abuse. Some of these people may be employed in the Armed Forces, or a nuclear power station, or flying a Jumbo jet!

CANADA

The Canadians, with about ten percent of the population of America, pay out an estimated $C10,000,000,000 (£4,761,000,000) to the drug traffickers. In 1986 one estimate gave Canada approximately 22,000 heroin addicts, 260,000 cocaine users, and at least 1½ million regular users of marijuana, all of them contributing to the $C 10 billion calculated above. Even a country as rich as Canada can ill afford such an immense leakage of wealth from her economy.

EUROPEAN ECONOMIC COMMUNITY

The worldwide cost of £207,000,000,000 is ten times the budget of the whole EEC. The community is made up of some 320 million people, and it is not unrealistic to think that the European Community may be spending just as much on illegal drugs as the United States. What *is* known is that the estimated number of heroin addicts in the Community is one and a half million, about 200,000 of them in Britain, each of whom spends, on average, £50 per day for drugs. £50 per day for one and a half million addicts adds up to £75,000,000 per day, or £27,375,000 a year out of the Community's economy for heroin alone. Incidentally, £27,375,000,000 is about £7 billion more than the entire EEC budget.

UNITED KINGDOM

The amount paid over to the drug barons by Britain's heroin addicts alone, based on the figures given above, will be £3,650,000,000, a sum equal to the cost of building 121,666 council houses at £30,000 each!

However, heroin users represent only about one fifth of Britain's drug addict population; there are also those who use cocaine, cannabis, barbiturates, hallucinogens, etc. How much is spent on these other drugs of abuse is not known for certain, but it may be possible to work out how much it could be from some estimates. As a rule of thumb, the United Kingdom Customs and Excise Department is generally believed to intercept and seize about 10 per cent of the drugs which smugglers try to bring into the country. Therefore, in 1985, the Customs Preventive Service seized 79kg of cocaine. This would suggest that about 711kg may have entered the country at a wholesale price of about £12,500 per kilo, equal to a total of £10.6 million. Cocaine is usually diluted to 20 per cent purity, so the kilo becomes worth about £62,500, and the 711kg worth about £44,437,500.

Again, in 1985, the customs seized 13,314kg of herbal cannabis and 7,089kg of cannabis resin. Herbal cannabis is worth about £2,000 a kilo on the streets, and resin, about £8,000 a kilo. Because of its bulk and very strong smell, the percentage of cannabis seized is usually higher than that of any other drug – about twenty-five per cent; this would suggest that 39,942kg of herbal cannabis and 21,267kg of cannabis resin may have entered the country. The total estimated value of this quantity of drugs would be approximately £250,000,000. Based on these estimates, the total cost for cocaine, herbal cannabis, and cannabis resin in 1985 would have been £294,457,500. If the same quantity entered Britain the following year, then the costs would be no greater than in 1985 for cocaine, herbal cannabis, and cannabis resin approximately (£294,457,500). However, if you add to this the estimated 1986 cost for heroin, £3,650,000,000, the grand total just for these four drugs amounts to £3,944,457,500 – nearly £4 billion.

These amounts of money are so enormous that they baffle ordinary people, as though someone were talking of light years in space, so it can help to relate the figures to something most people know about – Band Aid. Bob Geldof and his friends worked long and hard and raised £50 million for the poor, the thirsty, and the starving in Africa through the Band Aid fund drive. The drug barons worldwide put roughly that amount into their pockets every 2hr 6min, and every penny came from the misery of the millions of addicts around the world and the people they burgled, mugged, robbed, and murdered to get it.

All money made through the illicit drugs trade may be confiscated by British courts of justice, and may also be used in evidence in any prosecutions for drugs offences. Because of this, drugs traffickers move their money out of the country as quickly as they can. None of this money returns to the British economy and its removal is like a constantly bleeding wound, costing jobs, damaging businesses, affecting the value of the pound on the foreign exchanges, and creating other adverse social effects. Again, a comparison can help to make some of the cost understandable. Imperial Chemical Industries is one of the world's biggest and most efficient chemical companies, earning large amounts of money which contribute to the British economy. The chairman of ICI said recently, on a television programme, that his company traded about £1 million every hour throughout the year. From the figures estimated above, as the cost of buying illicit drugs, it would appear that the drug traffickers are stealing, from Britain's economy, about 46 pence out of every £1 put into it by ICI!

All of this money has come from drug addicts, but most of them are either unemployed or employed in low paid jobs. The conclusion must be that, apart from prostitution, most of this money is gained by theft. Cheating, stealing, mugging, robbery, burglary, shoplifting and petty theft are the main sources of the addict's funds, and this represents a tremendous cost to honest ordinary people. As drug abuse has increased, so have the crime statistics, to the extent that it is estimated that 50 per cent of all arrests made in the EEC are drug related. It may be, as some people claim, that the rise in the crime rate is a result of the high rate of unemployment and not drugs, but the ordinary man in the street wil probably find that hard to believe. No one knows for certain the full costs of the theft of money and goods carried out to provide the money for addicts to buy their drugs. Many people do not even trouble to report thefts to the police other than those whose goods are insured and must report the crime in order to claim on their insurance companies.

Most of the crimes of theft, housebreaking, muggings, burglaries, etc, are committed in working-class areas and housing estates. Well-policed suburbs with neighbourhood watch schemes and wealthy areas with burglar alarm systems on every house are usually avoided. It is the residents of the poorest and most deprived areas who are, in the main, having to pay for the addict's indulgence in drugs. The value of goods stolen must be enormous. Receivers of stolen goods rarely pay more than 10 per cent of the value of anything bought, and usually no more than 5 per cent for property such as transistor radios or stereo sets. The losses sustained by the public must be, therefore, enormous.

Crimes of theft are certainly rising at a rate that is forcing insurance companies to look to increased premiums and no-claim bonus schemes, to recover the costs of their ever rising payouts to clients who have been victimised. Householders of all classes are spending greater and greater amounts on locks, bolts, bars, alarms, reinforced doors, and house protection systems. Shopowners and businessmen are being forced virtually to fortify their premises. Private security companies are multiplying at an ever increasing rate, and armoured cars collecting cash from businesses and shops are equally common in British and American high streets. Vehicle manufacturers are being forced to instal more complex locks on car doors and boots as stolen cars and thefts from cars reach epidemic proportions, costing more than £260,000,000 annually. For example, one very popular tourist city in northwest England had more than 300 thefts from automobiles in one holiday weekend. Housebreakings are now so common that some people are afraid to leave their homes while they go away for a holiday without arranging for caretakers to live in until they return.

The cost of all this is very high for every citizen and it is very likely that it will get higher still. A major proportion of theft is almost certainly directly linked to the drug addicts' need for money to buy drugs. In 1983 it is estimated that there were approximately 140,000 heroin addicts in the United Kingdom. In 1986 the number was estimated at 200,000, a rise of 30 per cent in three years. A similar increase occurred in the USA, mainly in the use of crack. The cost to the country and to private individuals is an important factor which must be kept in mind in any consideration of the subject of drug addiction.

REPUBLIC OF IRELAND

About one in five of Ireland's population of 3,480,000 live in the capital, Dublin, and in Dublin alone there are an estimated 7,000 drug addicts mainly living in sprawling housing estates. The number of addicts in the country as a whole might be conservatively estimated as in excess of 21,000, but the inclusion of occasional marijuana users would raise this figure by at least 35,000. Of the addicts in Dublin, at least one third, some 2,400 are addicted to heroin and evidence indicates that they need to have between £100 and £200 per day to feed their habit. This would indicate that between £240,000 to £480,000 goes to the drug traffickers every day in Dublin from heroin addicts alone. The sum of £87,600,000 to

£175,200,000 per year for Dublin's heroin is made worse when considered in the context of Ireland's continuing struggle with severe economic and social problems. Even the EEC estimate of £50 per day for a heroin addict would give the Irish government cold comfort; they would still be losing £43,800,000 a year to the heroin dealers from Dublin alone!

Cannabis is the next most abused drug followed by Diconal and Physeptone (methadone) but there is chilling evidence of an increase in the availability of cocaine. The Irish Police (Garda) Drug Squad recently seized 293.17 grammes of cocaine sufficient to provide 45,236 'hits' at a street price of £10 a 'hit', after being diluted to 10 per cent purity. This seizure alone, at a street value of £452,360, probably saved the Irish people more than the cost of their drug squad for a whole year!

A matter of greater concern to Ireland's neighbours must be the recent seizure of 8,694 cannabis plants and 1,520 opium plants in the Republic. Ireland is justly famous for the richness of its agriculture and its temperate climate, conditions ideally suited to the cultivation of marijuana and opium poppies, and many of the country's farmers face poverty and ruin as a result of recent EEC moves to reduce the cost of the common agricultural policy. It would be tragic if these bureaucratic economies tempted farmers into the drug growing business. An acre of hay or potatoes is worth little nowadays. An acre of land planted with marijuana can produce approximately 2¾ tons of the drug which can be sold for £200–£300 per pound, providing a net return of between £1,232,000 and £1,848,000 per acre.

AUSTRALIA

Australia's 16 million people are widely envied for their high standard of living and the beauty, bounty, space, and climate of their huge country. This may be especially the case in Southeast Asia from where most of Australia's heroin addicts are supplied. A reasonable estimate of their numbers in 1986 would put a figure of some 60,000 regular users (although some estimates would put that figure on the low side) who paid approximately $A3,600,000,000 (£1,714,000,000) for their heroin. As in many other countries, cocaine is becoming more popular, aided by the glamour given to the drug by films, television, and the media generally. Most of the cocaine used has traditionally arrived in Australia via the Pacific Coasts of the USA and Canada but some may now be slipped in via Europe as a response to heightened vigilance on vessels and aircraft arriving by the Pacific route. Using Spain as an entry point to the whole of Europe the drug traffickers can utilise means of transportation to Australia which are less likely to be suspected by the authorities of carrying cocaine. There may now be as many as an estimated 29,000 cocaine users in Australia who may spend $A91,687,512 (£43,660,720) for their drug.

It must be a matter of grave concern to many Australians that officialdom pays little or no attention to marijuana use and rarely troubles to enforce the legislation that does exist. Marijuana is also being grown widely within Australia with little, or nothing, being done to prevent it. No one knows for certain how many people in Australia are marijuana users, and estimates vary too widely to be used. What is certain is that marijuana is implicated again and again in America and Europe as the 'gateway' drug to the use of heroin and cocaine, in as many as 30 per cent to 59 per cent of cases! Unless the Australian authorities take action now to curb the abuse of marijuana they may find that the present heroin and cocaine addiction figures will look miniscule within five years!

NEW ZEALAND

New Zealand's population of some 3,200,000 people are inherently conscious of their geographical isolation and some take pride in it. Many take equal pride in their country's long history of social justice and its traditional role of leading the world in now commonly accepted concepts such as votes for women, manhood suffrage, universal education, etc.

It may be, however, that this same isolation has misled some of the people in authority into thinking that their country is equally distanced from the plague of drug addiction currently sweeping over the rest of the world and this could prove very damaging to New Zealand.

Much attention has been focused on the abuse of alcohol, especially by the country's 352,000 Maoris, but there is some evidence of the growth of drug abuse other than drink.

There is some external evidence that suggests there could be an estimated 4,000 heroin users in New Zealand spending approximately $NZ196,370,000 (£73,000,000) a year on their drug, the equivalent of a levy of $NZ61 (£24) on every New Zealand citizen! Marijuana is easily available, widely used, and easily grown in some of the country's more remote areas.

EASTERN BLOC COUNTRIES

It has been almost a tradition for some marxist and socialist politicians to characterise drug abuse as an aberration arising from capitalist social conditions. It would seem that this particular claim may have to be revised as evidence emerges from the Communist states that they too are experiencing a rise in drug abuse among their young people. The evidence about this is still slight but it is there. This is no cause for pleasure on the part of even the most ardent anti-communist, it merely serves to emphasise the fact that drug abuse is a truly international evil and that those who traffic in drugs are the enemies of all of mankind.

USSR

Hundreds of thousands of young Russian conscript soldiers have now seen service in Afghanistan and many of them have returned to the Russian Motherland accustomed to smoking heroin of 60 per cent to 90 per cent purity. Many others have become hooked on Afghanistan's marijuana which is in plentiful supply and easily obtained, like heroin, in exchange for a few bullets. The Soviet authorities are so concerned about this they have cut postings to Afghanistan to only nine months for some personnel. Mr Gorbachov, has been responsible for more apparent change in Russia than any of his predecessors since the Revolution. Most startling of all, perhaps, is his attack upon the Russian tradition of vodka drinking to excess. He may be equally forthright in dealing with drug abuse and this could present the Western democracies with the opportunity to test out the new openness with joint action against the drug traffickers, perhaps even dealing with the Bulgarian drug processors!

POLAND

Poland with a population of over 36 million is also experiencing drug problems. More than 300,000 of Poland's young people are using opiate drugs obtained from locally grown poppies. There is no evidence of heroin use, but Polish addicts have developed a method of concentrating the juice from poppy tops; this increases the percentage of morphine in the resulting liquid, which is then injected. They are also using a method, similar to that used in Southeast Asia when processing opium, by which they can obtain liquid from the heads, stalks, and leaves of the poppy. A standard glass of this can contain up to 4.5 grains of morphine in about 0.25 litre of liquid. The longer this solution is boiled the stronger the morphine solution in the remaining liquid. It is not known for certain how many young Poles are using marijuana but it should be borne in mind that hemp, like the poppies, grows widely in Poland.

HUNGARY & JUGOSLAVIA

Both countries have rising numbers of drug addicts using heroin, marijuana, and other drugs. Neither the Iron Curtain nor clashing ideologies can be allowed to obstruct joint action against the drug barons.

THE PEOPLES REPUBLIC OF CHINA

For over a hundred years the very word China was synonymous with opium and opium smokers. From the 1930s onwards, with its introduction by the Japanese, heroin rapidly enslaved millions of Chinese. The drug traffickers made astronomical fortunes and China's economy and people suffered before an uncaring world. All this ended in October 1949 with the victory of the communist Peoples Liberation Army and the coming to power of the Chinese Peoples Government (CPG). With characteristic efficiency and necessary ruthlessness the CPG ended the drug trade in China. Notorious drug barons were shot and their property and fortunes confiscated. Those in the lower ranks of the drug trade were sent off to rehabilitation camps and those who obdurately refused to mend their ways were shot or fled to Hong Kong. Drug addicts were given the 'cold turkey' treatment and could not in any case obtain drugs. Again many fled to Hong Kong, giving rise to its unique drug problem.

With the exception of those opium poppies grown under strict supervision for medicinal purposes all opium cultivation was suppressed. China became, and remains, totally free of drug addiction. Any Chinese citizen who wishes to celebrate and perhaps get a little high may do so with fiery Chinese rice wine, or one of China's wines or spirits, or even some of the excellent Tsingtao beer . . . but that is all. There may be a lesson for the rest of the world in the determination with which the CPG stamped out China's greatest social evil!

4 Growth, manufacture and supply

PRODUCING COUNTRIES

There are seven countries which produce most of the world's illicit opium from which heroin and the other opium-based drugs, prepared opium, morphine, and codeine, are made. These countries are: Iran, Afghanistan, and Pakistan, in Southwest Asia – the 'Golden Crescent'; Burma, Laos, and Thailand in Southeast Asia – the 'Golden Triangle'; and Mexico. In 1983/84 they produced between 1,223 and 1,573 metric tons of the drug. A great deal of opium is prepared and used for smoking in opium pipes, mainly in Asia. However, if manufactured into heroin it would produce between 48 and 300 metric tons depending on the morphine content of the opium. It is estimated that just over 4 metric tons of this particular crop's heroin went to the United States and between 4 and 6 metric tons to Western Europe.

The opium poppy is a quite hardy plant which may be grown in a variety of climatic conditions from the subtropics to as far north as Manchuria. One requirement is, however, that the climate should be dry for the period of harvest which usually takes from 10 to 15 days. Traditionally, the opium poppy was grown on small plots of land farmed by a peasant and his family, but there is much evidence now of large scale cultivation with rotation of crops. It has even been alleged that some of the fertilisers, insecticides, equipment and irrigation schemes, supplied through international agencies to help the peasants grow substitute cash crops, have been used instead to improve yields of opium poppies.

The average yield of opium from any given number of plants may vary from 9kg per hectare (2.2 acres) in Turkey to 19kg per hectare in India and Burma. During harvesting, the seed capsules of the opium poppy are deeply scored and they exude a milky juice which hardens on exposure to the air. This material contains morphine and the morphine content falls with each repeated lancing of the capsules. When processed later, the hardened material is usually boiled, and impurities, such as bits of seed capsule case, removed.

Morphine is extracted from the opium by processing it in illegal laboratories which are sometimes portable. The morphine content of opium can vary from 5 to 20 per cent. Heroin is then derived from the morphine in a process which requires the use of complicated precursor chemicals and other chemicals such as acetic anhydride and ether to break down the original substance. It is not unusual, at this stage of processing, for illegal laboratories to blow up. The chemists who make the morphine and heroin are frequently addicts themselves and, while sampling their own products, become careless in the handling of dangerous chemicals. Ether, for example, is highly volatile and explosive. One such laboratory, concealed in a prestigious block of flats in Hong Kong, only came to official attention when the front of the building was blown out by ether fumes which escaped down a bathroom drain pipe and came into contact with a burning cigarette end! Heroin can be manufactured almost anywhere and laboratories are easily set up.

The only time that chemists are prevented from making morphine and heroin is when they are unable to obtain precursor chemicals which can only be produced by highly complex processes in large chemical plants. These chemicals and others such as acetic anhydride and ethyl ether, are essential for the manufacture of heroin and cocaine, and lack of them prevents the production of these drugs. Many of the laboratories are situated in jungle areas but many more are sited in western industrialised countries; some of the best known are in the region of Marseilles in France, others are in Italy and some, quite openly, are in several Communist countries.

Three countries grow almost all of the world's coca plants from which cocaine is made; they are Peru, Bolivia, and Colombia, in Latin America. The coca plants grow well in hot damp areas and they also flourish on drier hillsides in western Latin America. The plant is usually harvested when the leaves break on being bent. Leaves to be used for chewing are picked and dried in the sun, then kept in damp sacks to preserve their quality. Leaves for processing into cocaine are picked, and then reduced to coca paste by a crude process; the paste is then refined and purified in illegal laboratories. It takes about 200 metric tons of coca leaves to make one metric ton of coca paste, and about 2½ metric tons of coca paste to make one metric ton of cocaine. Illegal cocaine laboratories are easily set up and operated; some are transportable like mobile homes.

Laboratories are in operation in the producer countries and have also been found elsewhere, in countries such as Argentina, Brazil, Panama, Ecuador and Mexico. The laboratories are so simple to set up and operate that they can be created anywhere – Latin America, the Caribbean region, North America, and Europe. This is happening and will continue to happen as long as coca is grown and precursor chemicals are obtainable. In 1984, the producer countries grew 120,880 metric tons of coca leaf – over one third more than in the previous year. Yet in 1983 the drug dealers exported between 54 and 71 metric tons of cocaine to the United States and still had enough left over to send about 20 metric tons to Europe and elsewhere. Production has steadily increased to the point where dealers are actively searching for new markets and are offering cutprice cocaine as an incentive to potential buyers. Every indication suggests very strongly that their main target for increased cocaine sales is within the European Economic Community.

The hemp plant, source of herbal cannabis, hashish resin, and hashish oil, can be grown in almost any country temperate or tropical. The countries most involved in the growing of hemp for illicit purposes are well known. They are: Colombia, Jamaica, Mexico, Belize, Brazil, Panama, Venezuela, Costa Rica and the United States of America, in the Americas. It is generally accepted that the American crop is sold domestically, while the others are grown for export.

Indonesia and Thailand in Southeast Asia, Pakistan in Southwest Asia, Lebanon in the Middle East, Morocco in North Africa, and Nigeria in West Africa, are the other major growers for export. It is generally believed that the most potent hemp for drug purposes is that which is grown in a hot dry climate. Herbal cannabis is made from the crushed leaves, flowering tops, even twigs and seeds of the hemp plant, which have been dried for smoking. Hashish is a concentrated resin manufactured from the leaves and flowers of the plant. Hashish oil is an alcoholic extract of cannabis produced by a chemical process. It is known that some hashish oil has been manufactured in chemical works in Bulgaria from hemp grown in the Bekaa Valley in Lebanon. The world production of hemp (cannabis) in 1984 is estimated to have been between 16,030 and 18,880 metric tons; all of it for illicit sale and illicit use.

Almost every one of the countries with the climate and conditions suitable for growing drug crops, to supply drug addicts, is growing them. The profits being made so easily, at such low costs, are huge. In just one of the countries producing cocaine, Bolivia, the profits from the illicit drug traffic in 1984 were more than US$1¼ billion (£862 billion); the country's Gross National Product for that year was US$2½ billion, more than half of which came from the sale of drugs. Other countries that were not drug producers in the past have seen how easily the money is made without any risks, and these are now joining the drug trade.

Each member of the governments of the drug growing countries knows that drugs are being exported from his country to other countries for sale. Each knows that the main targets of the drug barons are the young people of the western nations, who have the money to buy illicit drugs, or who are prepared to get the money in any way they can. Each knows that illicit drugs are the cause of misery and hardship everywhere. Even the producing countries are beginning to be affected as their own people fall victim to drug addiction. The governments are arrogant in their corruptly made wealth and in their contempt for the strong nations that can do nothing to stop them at present. These legislators are agents of the merchants of death.

PACKAGING AND TRANSPORTING DRUGS

Opium, heroin and morphine

The opium-based drugs which arrive on Britain's streets in the form of heroin begin their journey by a network of footpaths and mule tracks winding their way from sometimes isolated farms and hamlets throughout Southeast and Southwest Asia. Although much of it comes from the remote small and scattered fields cultivated by peasant families in hidden valleys, far more is being grown on a large scale to cope with the ever rising demand being created in the industrialised nations. In addition to the increased consumption in the western countries, there is rising consumption in the producer countries and in all of the countries that the drugs pass through on their way to the main markets.

Representatives of the drug barons collect the raw opium and transport it to processing centres, usually by truck, although it is not uncommon for traditional mule trains to be used. The opium is then manufactured into morphine from which heroin is made. The best known high quality morphine is the '999' brand from Thailand; usually it is made up into compressed blocks. The heroin may be processed in the same secret laboratories, or the morphine may be sold for processing elsewhere. Heroin is generally transported wrapped in plastic.

Once manufactured, the drugs for export begin the long journey to their destinations. Some go via local seaports and airports to Europe, America, and Australasia but much goes via Burma and India. The traditional routes through Malaysia and Singapore are no longer popular. This loss of popularity has come about because the governments of those countries have introduced the death penalty for drug smuggling in a determined drive to stamp out drug addiction. They have been criticised for this by some liberal western Europeans, but it is certainly having some effect. Couriers are paid to carry some of the drugs as passengers on air flights which originate in cities some distance from the drug producing states. Drug couriers used to be paid from £5,000 to £10,000 depending on the risk involved but, as more countries impose heavier penalties for drug smuggling, the price is reportedly going up.

Large quantities of heroin may be concealed in just about every container imaginable. Drugs have been found by customs officers in dolls, furniture, vases, refrigerators, washing machines, huge containers from container lorries, in packets of detergent, and even inside dead bodies being sent home for burial. The drugs are always heavily guarded whenever they are moved or stored in the country of origin, or in neighbouring countries. Many of the guards are soldiers or policemen working for corrupt officers who, in turn, are usually working with corrupt politicians. Violence is an integral part of the drug trade and every step of the drugs' journey has a history of murder. All drug shipments are consigned to dealers in the country of destination by arrangements made through a middleman.

Cocaine

The situation in the cocaine producing countries of Latin America is much the same as that in the opium growing countries. Coca leaf is gathered and then processed into coca paste which is later refined into cocaine. The principal target for all cocaine is the United States of America, but increased areas of coca bush under cultivation have produced such abundant crops that production has outrun demand. There is, therefore, a big sales drive on in the search for new markets. Europe is the main target but Australia and New Zealand, because of their wealth, are also attractive to the drug barons. Again, as with all drugs, the profits to be made are enormous. Some idea of how rich the drug barons are can be gained from an offer to the American government by one of Bolivia's biggest drug traffickers, to personally pay off Bolivia's foreign debt of approximately £2½ billion, if his son were released from US custody! Aircraft, boats, trucks, cars – anything that can carry the cocaine is pressed into service to get the drug to America. An aircraft can make one flight into the USA and then crash; so long as the drugs can be unloaded and moved, it does not matter since the profit on that one cargo is sufficient to buy 100 other aeroplanes.

Couriers, also known as 'mules', may carry the drug wrapped in plastic or contained in a contraceptive sheath inside their bodies. The drug is either swallowed or inserted into one of the body's openings. Some have already died when the package wrapping split and released the drug into the carrier's system. It has been reported that even babies have been used for this purpose.

Cocaine comes mainly to Europe from Colombia, Peru, and Bolivia, and the main transit centres are Rio de Janeiro and São Paulo in Brazil, Montevideo in Uruguay, and Buenos Aires in Argentina. Frankfurt, Copenhagen, Amsterdam, Madrid, and Lisbon are the main entry points in Europe. There is some evidence to indicate that Spain may be the most popular country for the illicit importation of cocaine into Europe. Many Latin Americans speak Spanish and have longstanding, legitimate business links. There are easy routes to Spain via the Canary Islands with many sailings and there are regular air flights between Spain and Latin America. An added attraction for the smuggler is that the maximum penalty in Spain for smuggling drugs is 12 years, reduced to 6 years for good behaviour, and there is no confiscation of the smuggler's assets. The penalty for trafficking offences in the United Kingdom is life imprisonment with no parole given, and all assets confiscated.

Herbal cannabis, hashish resin, and hashish oil

Cannabis can be grown almost anywhere; it has even been discovered growing inside an apartment in a building in New York. Because of this wide area of possible cultivation, it can come into Europe and America from any direction. A huge quantity is grown in the USA but demand for it is so great that thousands of tons still have to be smuggled in to satisfy the millions of American users.

Much of the cannabis coming in to Europe is brought from North Africa and the Lebanon. Most of it is from Morocco, and the short sea-crossing to Spain makes it relatively easy for smugglers to import their cargoes. There are large numbers of small boats in the sea areas around the Spanish coast and, during the holiday period, fishermen are outnumbered by yachtsmen. This, plus the large number of tourists in transit through Spain to and from Morocco, makes the task of the Spanish anti-drug squads almost impossible. The strong smell given off by herbal cannabis and its bulk make it a far less profitable drug to smuggle than heroin or cocaine. Its undeserved reputation for being harmless, however, means that there is a huge, seemingly insatiable market waiting to buy it, so that profits are good for a comparatively small outlay of money. Hashish resin and hashish oil are smaller in bulk, easier to seal into containers (which reduce the odour), and are much easier to hide when in transit. Any large cargo of strong smelling materials may conceal herbal cannabis, and shipping containers are one of the favoured means of transportation throughout Europe and into the UK. The chances of being caught are slight because of the volume of container traffic.

The customs officers at Dover are among the most experienced and hardest working of their breed in the world, yet even they can search only a fraction of the 300,000 or more containers which pass through their hands in an average year.

THE RISKS TO DRUG CARGOES

The drug barons have little fear of ever becoming poor. A bag of heroin weighing one kilogram, the size of a bag of sugar, can be bought in Asia for approximately £12,000. The same bag of heroin can sold in Britain for at least £130,000 and, if diluted, for twice or three times that amount. With profits like these the drug traffickers can afford to lose eight out of ten shipments and still show a profit; all of the signs indicate that they do not lose more than one shipment in ten. The drug trade is totally international; the traffickers and their employees ignore all frontiers. They have agents and financial experts working right round the clock on their behalf. Drug dealers are in every town and city in Europe ready and willing to sell their products. More and more people are taking drugs and more misinformation is being spread about drugs.

Customs and police officers are balked at every frontier by outmoded national procedures. Even within the UK the drug squad from one police area will be most reluctant to trespass into another police area without time-wasting arrangements being made. Law enforcement agencies are kept short of funds and personnel for anti-drugs activities. Some police chiefs do not regard drug squad detectives as proper policemen, nor do they see anti-drugs work as proper police work. Drugs prosecutions take long and careful preparation and some chief constables want quick results. What this all means is that there are few risks to drug cargoes.

5 Drugs in History

The history of mankind is also a history of men's desire to eat or drink things that make them feel euphoric. Farming began about 6000BC, more than likely closely followed by home-brewing. By the time of the reign of King Hammurabi of Babylonia (2067–2025BC), the sale and consumption of alcohol was evidently well known, as he tried to regulate drinking houses in Babylon.

Later, in the first century AD, the Romans tried to reduce wine production without much success. Herbs, roots, mushrooms and other fungi, as well as alcoholic beverages were either drunk, eaten, rubbed on the skin, or inhaled, to achieve euphoric, exalted, trancelike states: sometimes this was done as part of religious rites, to see visions of to gain insights, as in Shamanism; sometimes in initiation ceremonies to dull the pain of ritual mutilation. Sometimes these rites were performed to give warriors greater strength and pain resistance in battle or to programme them to kill, like the Hashishin, or the assassins; sometimes they were used as pain and hunger suppresents, or to help to cope with the thin air at high altitudes as in the Andes. But also, sometimes they were done just to relax during celebrations. This was all very well, and not too harmful generally, until mankind learned to increase the power and effects of his euphorics, by distillation of the alcohol into strong spirits, and by the extraction of the euphoric chemicals from the plants.

Opium

The history of China gives a dreadful warning of the awful consequences that can befall even a rich nation if the dangers of widespread drug abuse are ignored. The Chinese example is a very apt demonstration of what could happen to any of the countries under threat today from the drug barons. The men who were responsible for China's agony were respectable British businessmen and the direct cause was opium.

Opium is obtained from the seed capsule of the opium poppy. The original home of the wild opium poppy is believed to have been in the region of the Eastern Mediterranean and from there it spread east and west. There is evidence that some knowledge of the opium poppy reached China by about AD700 and it was widely used as a medicine from then until the 17th century when some Chinese traders introduced a peculiar Dutch habit.

Early in the 17th Century, Dutchmen in the trading areas in Java, Indonesia, began taking a pinch of opium with their pipes of tobacco to induce a mild relaxation and sense of wellbeing. Chinese traders doing business with the Dutch observed this habit and copied it. For some reason, which is still not fully understood, the Chinese became enthusiastic about this practice and indulged in it more and more.

The Chinese began progressively reducing the quantity of tobacco and increasing the amount of opium until, finally, the tobacco was dispensed with and only pure opium was smoked in pipes specially made for that purpose. Inhaled, the smoke from these pipes introduced the narcotic via the lungs immediately into the bloodstream where it quickly acted upon the brain.

This opium smoking habit was introduced into China and spread rapidly throughout the whole country. By the early 1800s it has been estimated that about 10 per cent of China's population was addicted to opium smoking (approximately 30 million people), and the effects on the country were disastrous. Some missionary reports of the time told of whole districts with crops and animals, even the children, neglected, the countryside and fields uncultivated and unattended, and villages littered with the bodies of opium addicts lost in drug-induced dreams amidst great squalor.

The social effects of the opium trade were bad enough, but the economic effects were worse. For thousands of years China had had a balanced economy with no inflation and no trade debts. Except for periods of flood, drought, or famine, the country was stable economically, if not politically. China's industry effectively served her needs and there was little demand for goods from abroad. British manufactured goods were on the whole clumsy when compared to the Chinese products. Even British textiles, which sold well everywhere else, were derided by the Chinese as harsh and barbaric compared to their own silks and other materials. In the original trade between Britain and China the balance of trade was always in favour of the Chinese; in one period the Chinese bought only £9 million of goods from Britain while the British paid £26 million for tea. Opium addiction changed this.

By the mid-19th century British traders were taking half of China's total annual revenue for opium sales and, by the 1870s, they were culling an even greater amount. The disgraceful exploitation of the Chinese by the British drug barons bankrupted the country, killed millions of Chinese people, involved Britain in two opium wars, and caused social, economic, and moral disruption that lasted for nearly one hundred years until 1949.

The horrible fate of China and its suffering people must be kept in mind when persuasive and deceiving arguments are put forward by promoters of the campaign for legalisation of drug abuse. Even though the drug barons of Peru, or Afghanistan are unlikely to declare war on the western nations to force their drugs upon them, the effects of widespread drug taking are just as exhausting and economically disastrous as warfare.

By the 19th century opium was freely available in Britain and very popular in the form of an alcoholic solution called laudanum. The Victorian public indulged itself in huge quantities of patent medicines whose main active ingredient was morphine. Babies were helped to sleep or kept quiet with drinks made from infusions of poppy seeds and poppy heads; some were even quietly murdered with laudanum for small amounts of insurance money. The country was awash with opium and morphine and no-one was particularly worried. The main concern of the churches, particularly the reformist evangelical churches, and of the self-appointed guardians of the nation's morals was not drug addiction, which was the domain of the rich and the upper middle class, but 'demon drink', the beer and spirits drunk by the working classes. Times do not seem to have changed; much the same sort of people are now comparing alcohol unfavourably with cannabis!

Morphine was first processed from opium in 1806 and was considered a gift from God for its pain-relieving properties; the most powerful and effective drug of its kind. It was only after considerable use that it was seen to be highly addictive. The invention of the hypodermic syringe in the mid-19th century meant that addicts could handily inject themselves with morphine, and later, with heroin. Heroin was derived from morphine in 1874 and was produced 25 years later by a German pharmaceutical company as a cough medicine under the trade name Heroin. It was originally believed that heroin was from 4 to 8 times more powerful than morphine and it was introduced as a substitute for morphine as it was thought to be less addictive; in fact, it is far more highly addictive than morphine and the addiction is even harder to cure.

HEMP (*Cannabis sativa*)

The hemp plant is the source of marijuana and hashish. it is thought to have originated in a region north of the Himalayan mountains. Ancient writings indicate that it was used for its fibres in China in 2800BC. It is supposed that the plant spread from Asia to Eastern and Southern Europe, and had reached Western Europe by AD500. Hemp was introduced to the New England states and Virginia in about 1645. Its main use was for the manufacture of a wide range of products ranging from ropes to textiles. Hemp oil has been used in the manufacture of paints, varnish and soap, and hempseed has been much used in ready-mixed feed for caged birds. It was the rapid rise in sales of one particular brand of bird seed that alerted some American police to the fact that enthusiastic pot addicts had found they could legitimately buy a packet of seed and grow their own marijuana.

The history of hemp as a drug

The word 'assassin' passed into the English language as a term for someone who murders by treacherous violence. Crusaders returned from Syria with stories of the terrorist agents of the 'Old Man of the Mountains' who were given hashish to induce ecstatic visions of Paradise before setting out to face death and martyrdom. Certainly the 'Old Men of the Mountains' existed over a period of approximately a century and a half (1090–1256) when they were involved in an Islamic religious dispute. They even changed their religious doctrine to make the murder of enemies a sacred religious duty! From their strongholds, assassin terrorists and agents spread, murdering all those who were considered to be their enemies. They were finally brought down in 1273 by a double assault from the Mongols and a Syrian Mameluke general. Their modern successors are busily growing hemp in the Bekaa Valley of Lebanon today for sale in Europe. The names may have changed, but not the habits of terrorism.

Hemp as a drug today

Hemp has been eaten or smoked as a drug: in India where it is known as *bhang, charas* or *ghanga*; Egypt and Asia Minor where it is known as *hashish*; North Africa as *kif* or *kef*; and in the western countries where it is known mainly as *marijuana, pot, grass cannabis.*

There was some use of hemp as a drug in America before the 1960s where it is known as marijuana, but it was associated in the public mind with immigrants and the poor. It was prohibited in 1937 but there was little interest in it as a drug, possibly because it was not considered as glamorous, and did not figure to any extent in films or in the print media.

In the 1960s marijuana became popular with the 'hippie' drop-outs of America. Pop music, long hair and grass became the uniform trappings of the young, in rebellion against the bounty of affluent America. As with all American crazes, the British and other Europeans soon followed. Anti-war, anti-racism, anti-anything rallies, wreathed in pot-smoke, were major public activities in between pop concerts and public demonstrations of brotherly love. The myth of marijuana's harmlessness was actively promoted, and a whole generation switched on and went to pot. Marijuana is still widely consumed today, but reports from some of the reputable universities in America indicate that, in general, the intelligent students are avoiding all drugs, including cannabis. One survey in British universities indicated that approximately one third of the students had tried cannabis. Apart from the dangers of marijuana's mind-affecting chemicals, it is the drug with which most addicts seem to start before moving on to something even more potent. Its greatest danger may be as a gateway to addiction. Hemp is at the centre of the present attempt by some people to legalise drug use in the UK and other western countries. The claim is being made that it is comparatively harmless, and may even be not as harmful as traditional drinks, such as beer. This is dealt with elsewhere in this book. One hundred years ago there was a similar argument when it was decided by the medical profession that Heroin should be used for medicinal purposes in preference to morphine, since it was believed to be less addictive! In fact, it makes addicts more easily than morphine does, and the addiction is harder to cure.

COCAINE

In a poll taken in 1985 it was found that 15 million Americans had tried cocaine; all the indications are that the numbers are still rising. Overproduction in Latin America has caused a drop in price, and an aggressive sales campaign is being conducted by the cocaine dealers.

Cocaine is obtained from the leaves of the coca bush which is commonly found wild in Peru and Bolivia, but it is now also being widely cultivated in many other countries, and has even been introduced to Indonesia. For many centuries the Andean Indians of Latin America have chewed coca leaves, sometimes mixed with ashes of plants and limestone, for pleasure, and to enable them to tolerate strenuous activity at high altitudes where the air is thin. When taken by mouth, it anaesthetises the stomach so that hunger and thirst are not felt. The Incas and the Spanish colonisers had no more success in curbing the use of the coca leaf among the Indians than modern governments are having in curbing the use of cocaine today.

Cocaine's value as a local anaesthetic was first discovered in Vienna in 1884 and it has been used for that purpose extensively in operations on the ears, nose, throat and eyes, and for dentistry. As with opium, cocaine was used extensively by patent medicine manufacturers in a variety of concoctions guaranteed to cure all ills. It was sold over the counter incorporated into sprays, gargles and pills. In North America it was even used as one of the ingredients of the universally popular drink Coca-Cola until the early 1900s. Cocaine was known traditionally as the drug of the upper classes and the rich, a reputation that gave it a spurious glamour from the 1920s until the present day. The most dangerous myth about cocaine was that it could be used by the casual user, just for fun, as it was not supposed to be addictive. Many people have paid for believing this myth with ruined health, ruined lives and death.

The drug barons have put so much more land to the cultivation of the coca bush during the last few years that there is now overproduction; there is even too much for the North American market which consumed about 80 metric tons of cocaine in 1983. The amount is hardly surprising when it is now estimated that in the USA there are one million cocaine addicts, eight million regular users, and 20,000,000 people who use it from time to time. Now Europe and Australasia are the main targets for the surplus.

HALLUCINOGENS

Hallucinogens, such as LSD, are modern chemical drugs manufactured to imitate the sensations experienced by some people in bygone years when they consumed herbs, lichens, fungi, mushrooms of various kinds, and the peyote cactus, a native of Mexico and the USA.

Fungi have always seemed mysterious plants to Man. They appear quickly, seem to grow without roots and sustenance and then disappear without trace. They have figured in legends and myths from time immemorial. Fungi have been used as stimulants, narcotics and intoxicants in all sorts of ceremonies all over the world.

Tribal shamans in Northern Siberia are believed to have used preparations of the fly agaric mushroom to induce animated, excitable trances and visions in connection with their religious ceremonies. In Borneo and New Guinea, similar mushroom madness is deliberately induced in ceremonies and celebrations. In Mexico and Central America the native Indians used fungi which produced a hallucinogenic effect. Fungi have been used in ceremonies, religious rites, fertility rites, etc, for centuries and still are being used in some parts of the world.

Peyote is a spineless cactus which grows in Northern Mexico and in Texas. The properties are such that, when eaten, it produces extraordinary psychological and physiological effects. Before the 20th century, peyote was used as a medicine to induce visions of supernatural revelations. A religion of prayer and quiet contemplation centred on the peyote later developed – it is believed to have orginated in Oklahoma – and eventually it spread to all the American Indian tribes. Some groups practising the peyote religion formed the Native American Church in 1918.

The original ceremonial and religious uses of the natural hallucinogens were far removed from the 'trips' of the 1960s' hippie culture. The synthetic hallucinogen effect is well known now. Some of the more bizarre 'bad trips' reported from the USA have alerted most sensible people to the dangers of using the drug.

Mescaline

The extract from peyote, is only about a three thousandth of the strength of LSD and is generally reputed to give gentler and relatively safe trips. Unfortunately, most of the substances sold in Britain as mescaline are probably LSD.

6 The Future

The present havoc caused by traditional drug abuse is bad enough, but it looks as if worse is still to come. Like the transistor and the silicon chip, chemistry has advanced rapidly, and substances that would have needed a chemical complex for their manufacture just twenty years ago can now be made in a basement from a few chemicals which can be bought cheaply almost anywhere. This has happened in California already and it is just a question of time until it happens here. These new drugs are called 'analogue' or 'designer' drugs. They are created, usually by means of a computer which is programmed first to formulate new patterns of molecules and then to list which common chemicals will react to produce the necessary molecules.

The next step is to change the molecular pattern of some new synthetic drug, to make a different one that may have the effect of heroin but will not actually be heroin. It is like making up a fake heroin, which may look like heroin and may give all the effects of heroin, but is much cheaper than heroin and it is not, so far as the law is concerned, an illicit drug. A major problem with these designer drugs is that they are like the bath tub gin of the American prohibition era which looked and smelt like gin, but which could blind or kill. Similarly, the new drugs can paralyse and kill.

The best known designer drug so far is 3-methyl fentanyl which is a methyl analogue of fentanyl, a legitimate pain killing drug. Originally 3-methyl fentanyl was produced in a laboratory and is approximately 1,000 times stronger than heroin. But illicitly produced drugs are not made under strictly controlled conditions, nor are they tested for safety before sale. Consequently at least 100 heroin addicts died in California from taking a fake heroin known as China white. In another case, in 1982, a designer drug was made to copy a strong narcotic three times as powerful as morphine – MTPP. There was a slip-up in the manufacture and the 'synthetic heroin' which was produced was found to paralyse people; they could not move, nor could they talk, but they stayed alive. Later it was found that treatment similar to that given to victims of Parkinson's disease could help the victims. It was thought at first that this drug had been made by some top chemist, but it was later discovered to have been made by a student in a basement workshop. People will continue to make these analogue drugs because the profits can be enormous. £200 or $400 worth of chemicals can make up a batch of synthetic heroin worth $400,000,000 or £200,000,000, and drug addicts will buy it because they must have their fix whatever the dangers. It has been reasonably estimated that one fifth of the heroin being sold in California now is 3-methyl fentanyl.

Part III
Remedies

7 Legalisation & its consequences

It has been suggested by some political figures and some members of the 'caring professions', that drug addicts should not be treated as criminals; that they are, in fact, suffering from a chronic medical condition, albeit self-induced, similar to that of tobacco and alcohol users. The argument is that the criminalisation of drug addiction leads addicts into overt criminal and anti-social behaviour because they have no other means to obtain the drugs they must have. From this assumption follows the suggestion that the supply of drugs of addiction through the health service would result in the eradication of criminal and anti-social behaviour by addicts, and would see the withdrawal of criminal elements, such as the Mafia, the Chinese Triads etc, from the drugs traffic as there would be no profit in it for them.

This is a much simplified version of the general theory of the decriminalisation of drug addiction, but it contains the main theme of the 'chronic condition' lobby.

It may be that the originators and supporters of this proposition might be thought naive, to the point of idiocy, but this scheme is deserving of examination. A fair consideration of all aspects of law, administration, health, and family affairs would have to be made. If such a scheme were to be introduced, legislation would be essential.

THE ADDICT

The addict would have to be identified and certified as a bona fide addict, and would require to be registered and furnished with evidence of his status as a drug addict before qualifying for a free supply of his drug of addiction. It is at this introductory stage that the first problems of this scheme may be encountered. The majority of addicts, in any society, do not want to be identified as drug addicts; in fact, many of them would energetically reject the notion that they are addicts. Some would reject the notion for psychological reasons, some for social, family, religious, or employment reasons, and others for a simple rejection response to the idea of being so labelled.

Many addicts are juveniles, minors in the eyes of the law, and as such would require either parental approval or a court ruling before being included in any drug supply scheme. It is a matter of doubt whether any parents, or judges, would consider life as a State-supported drug addict a suitable future for any young person. Therefore, it must be presumed that those persons for whom the decriminalisation scheme is proposed, ostensibly as a benefit, are the very people who would avoid registration at all costs, since the fact of their addiction would necessarily be brought to the attention of their families and probably the public at large. If this proved to be the case, then the main foundation of the legalisation lobby's argument is removed – ie that legalisation would remove the profit motive from drug dealing. Far from the benefit claimed, this form of legalisation would, almost certainly, only be of use to the adult addicts. This would increase the pressure on traffickers to draw ever larger numbers of youngsters into the drug net, as they, together with some adults who would have personal or professional reasons for wishing to keep their addiction secret, would be the only market for illicit drugs.

ADDICTS AND LEGAL SUPPLIERS

A general point to consider must also be the nature of drug addiction and the tendency for addicts to find the need, through habituation, to continually increase quantities of any supplied drug, or combination of them. The administrators and medical personnel involved in such a legalised scheme would presumably have to be empowered by law to supply drugs on demand to addicts, even if the demands became borderline or sub-lethal dosages. They would also have to be granted advanced absolution from blame and legal process for drug-induced death at their hands, by a general exclusion from the homicide legislation pertaining in most societies. Even courts of law and independent coroners' inquests would have to be barred from verdicts suggesting any responsibility on the part of government officials operating a legal drug provision scheme. It may be that the public at large would have the gravest objections or reservations at any such legislation.

Yet it is no solution to suggest that the drug providers should limit the quantity supplied to addicts, as this would merely result in them returning to illicit sources for their additional supplies. This again undercuts the legalisation lobby's argument for removing the profit motive.

THE ADDICT AND SOCIETY

It must be presumed that society would demand certain minimal regulation and legislation in return for providing public money and other resources for the free supply of drugs to the addicts. The public would also have to be prepared to support the addicts financially through social security benefits since few, if any of them, would be fit or able to make a living. In any case it would be doubtful whether any employer would wish to employ an addict on a maintenance support system. Legislation and regulation would certainly have to be comprehensive enough to provide protection for the public against exploitation by addicts, and by those administering the programme.

REGISTRATION OF A DRUG ADDICT

Any drug addict wishing to obtain free drugs and financial support through a scheme administered by the health department would have to have his name recorded in a central register. He would also have to obtain a Registered Drug Addict's Entitlement & Identification Card. The registration card would have details of the addict: name; address; drug issue; national insurance number; card number; and it would bear the addict's signature and photograph. This card would have to be carried at all times, and would entitle the addict to his drug issue at pre-arranged places and times. The card would also identify the registered addict to his local unemployment office where his inclusion on a special file would ensure that he was not offered unsuitable work. Application for inclusion on the register would be made through health centres, drug treatment centres, doctors surgeries and hospitals.

An addict seeking registration would have to provide proof of his identity, age, and citizenship. Evidence of his addiction to particular drugs, or combinations of them, would also be required and this would, normally, be provided by a doctor, or the drug treatment centre. All the other personal information might be verified by some official or person of legal standing such as a doctor, police or probation officer, social worker or solicitor, as is currently done for passport applications.

ASSURANCES OF ADDICT'S ENTITLEMENTS

It would be guaranteed by government that registration would not be a ploy designed to force addicts to give up drug taking, or to undertake any treatment. This assurance would be necessary, as without it the scheme would not be accepted by addicts who would fear some deception to their disadvantage. However, this should not prevent any official or non-official body attempting to persuade addicts to give up drugs by means of advertising, or by persuasions similar to those used in anti-smoking campaigns. An addict's personal details would not be released to any such organisations. Government should also guarantee that there would be no reduction in the quality or quantity of the drugs supplied to the registered addict. It would have to be further assured that a request from an addict for an increased demand of drugs, as a result of his own increased consumption, would be approved. A larger dose would be provided after due warning of the possible consequences of the increased dosages, eg severe illness or death. In either event there would be no blame attached to the government or its officers, providing the warning had been given, and a form of release had been signed by the addict, before the issue of the stronger drugs. All the necessary equipment needed for drug-taking would also be supplied free, eg disposable syringes, saline solution etc.

COMPULSORY CONDITIONS FOR A REGISTERED ADDICT

1. A registered addict must carry his registration card at all times. This would be necessary in case he was found unconscious and unable to explain the cause of his condition.
2. A registered addict would have to have a permanent address, either private or institutional. This would be necessary for administration and for safety checks in the event of failure to appear for drug issues.
3. A registered addict would have to notify the registrar at least 72 hours before quitting his registered address, and within 72 hours of taking up his new residence.
4. Temporary absence from a registered address, for more than 6 days, would have to be notified. This would be necessary for keeping track of drug issues.
5. A registrar would have the authority to check that a registered addict's notified addresses were bona fide, and for this purpose would have the power to appoint any properly qualified person to act for him. The qualified persons being policemen, probation officers, social workers, or any such like persons with the knowledge and expertise suited to dealing with drug addicts.

SUPPLEMENTARY CONDITIONS OF REGISTRATION FOR PUBLIC PROTECTION

Once registered, an addict would have to comply with regulations and conditions imposed for the protection of the general public.

1. A registered addict would not be permitted to hold any licence, or any operator's permit, or vessel operator's permit, or pilot's licence, to operate, drive, control, or command any ship, boat, aeroplane, car, truck, bus, train, or any other vehicle, or conveyance, or mechanically operated machinery such as a fork-lift truck, JCB, or crane; whether used in a private or public place. This is essential for the safety of the public. No-one may be trusted with any of the above whilst taking drugs regularly.
2. A registered addict would not be allowed to hold any position of authority over, or responsibility for, any group or individual, either as a parent or guardian, foster parent, youth leader, or in

any other way. No-one taking drugs regularly may be trusted to carry out their duties in such positions at all times.

3. A registered addict would be barred from being a member of the armed forces, police, fire or ambulance services. The reasons for this ban are self-evident. No person taking drugs could be relied upon to handle weapons, act as a police officer, or to deal with emergencies.
4. A registered addict would be barred from working in any power station, chemical, pharmaceutical, or petroleum plant, or any other industry where his drug habit could prove dangerous to the public.
5. A registered addict would not have the right to sue any employer, or prospective employer, on the grounds of discrimination. The fact that a person is registered should be legitimate grounds for dismissal from any employment. An employer is entitled to expect his employees to be fit and capable of work at all times, other than in cases of genuine illness.
6. Registration would be legitimate grounds for divorce. No person should be forced to remain married to an addict.
7. Registration would be legitimate grounds for refusing custody of children in cases of divorce or separation. It would be wrong to entrust the care of children to a junkie.
8. Registration should be a bar to adoption.
9. Registration should be legitimate grounds for legal action to have wills and inheritances of all kinds changed by the courts. This would include control of property, trusts, funds, etc.

   The courts should be able to appoint fit persons as trustees or executors to look after the financial affairs of the addict. This would be to safeguard an addict's interests as he would be a target for exploitation.
10. Registration would be a legitimate reason for varying the usual rules of primogeniture or succession, ie, the inheritance of titles of nobility. An addict would certainly be incapable of carrying out his duties or managing the affairs which usually are required of such rank. The title would normally pass to the next in line of succession.
11. Registration would be a bar to membership of the nation's legislature or any public office.

12. Registration would be a bar to employment in any position or office which is subject to official secrecy or in any post where secrecy or confidentiality is essential – law, banking, etc.
13. Professional bodies and institutes, which operate registers for the authentication of their members' qualifications and fitness for the practice of their profession would have to strike any addicts from their lists. Failure to do so would make them liable in damages suits. It would be quite wrong for a medical association or any other body, knowingly to allow a member to practise whilst under the influence of drugs.
14. The fact of registration would have to be revealed in any application for bank or building society accounts, or mortgages, loans, or credit cards.
15. No registered addict would be permitted to be a trustee, treasurer, agent, or hold any post involving money or valuables.
16. A registered addict would not be allowed to have control of or responsibility for any animal.
17. An addict would be removed from the register on proof of a cure of his addiction, but a record of his previous registration would be retained.
18. The act of removal from the register would not necessarily mean an automatic cancellation or reversal of any decisions or judgements made by the courts during prior registration. The courts would not be compelled to change their previous judgements unless they deemed it safe to do so.
19. Any titles or professional standing would not be restored because of the former addict's removal from the register. The above list is far from comprehensive and many more instances would have to be reviewed.

GENERAL POINTS OF LAW APPLYING TO THE REGISTRATION OF ADDICTS

The fact that any person was registered as an addict would not absolve or excuse him from blame or responsibility for any crime, offence, or legal wrong done by him, whether under the influence of his drugs or not.

The fact that a registered addict receives his drugs from a government department would not render the government or its agents liable to being sued for anything done by the addict whilst under the influence of drugs.

Any private citizen would have the right to object to any addict or group of addicts living in or occupying any property owned by him, or in his place of business, or employment or in his home.

The rights of private citizens who are not drug addicts must not be diminished for the benefit of registered drug addicts. Without the general support of the public the scheme would fail.

The private citizen must have the right to object to the presence of large numbers of addicts living near his home, or the siting of drug supply stations near his home or place of business, or near a school.

THE POSITION OF REGISTRAR

The registrar would be appointed in Britain by the Lord Chancellor and in the US by his judicial equivalent. He would be the type of person whose public service, and legal or medical qualifications would make him suitable for the post.

Removal from the post, other than in the normal course of retirement, or resignation on the grounds of ill-health, shall be only by means of impeachment, conviction in a court for any serious offence, or if he shall be made bankrupt, or if he shall accept any other paid state office.

The salary and other conditions of service should be equivalent to that of a senior judge.

The registrar would have to be empowered to submit to the legislature any suggestions or recommendations for the variance, additions, cancellation, or amendments, to the legislation pertaining to the act; and any regulations, conditions and administrative instructions employed in the application of the act.

The nation's legislature would have to pass all necessary legislation for the act, its operation, the formation of the department and its finance and conditions of service, etc. However, as with the courts of justice, parliamentarians must not be empowered to interfere in the daily affairs of the drugs registry department.

DEPUTY REGISTRARS

The positions, responsibilities and conditions would be the same as for the registrar, but equivalent to lower court judges, ie quarters assizes judges.

PERSONAL VETTING & COUNTER-CORRUPTION PROVISIONS

It is common knowledge that the illegal traffic in drugs has created enormous profits for the drug barons, who seem to be able to enslave large numbers of people of all nationalities with virtual impunity. Their vast fortunes enable the drug traders to corrupt, not only individuals, but also members of governments which may not have the courage to attempt to curb the drug trafficking, as in the case of Bolivia. The amounts involved are astronomical. In some cases the drug barons have personal fortunes greater than the Gross National Product of some Third World countries.

Drugs and corruption are synonymous. This must be borne in mind when considering the very severe and intrusive conditions of service which would have to be accepted by the employees of the drugs registry. All employees, as officers in the department from the registrar down, would have to accept personal vetting of their private lives and their finances at irregular intervals throughout their period of service, and even for some time after leaving. Nothing less than the strictest safeguards would allay public suspicions. As nothing less than the utmost continual, proof of honesty and integrity within the department would guarantee public support for the scheme, it must follow, therefore, that salaries and other conditions of service would have to be commensurate with the severe loss of personal privacy experienced by departmental staff – very high salaries, generous vacations, and other perquisites, plus the right to early retirement. It would also be necessary to exclude such salaries and perks from consideration in any 'comparability' exercises carried out by trade unions or pay councils, as no other work could be comparable.

THE DRUGS REGISTRY

It can be seen that the department headed by the registrar would be very large and complex.

Its responsibilities would be nationwide, as the legislation on legalisation and registration could not be permitted any variations in its operations anywhere in the country. The registry would have such a variety of inter-related links with other departments, and the success of its operations would be of such importance that the registrar would have to have powers equal to those of the heads of every other government department. No one could be permitted to obstruct the work of the registry, not even the Treasury!

THE CONSEQUENCES OF LEGALISATION

It is easy to put forward attractive arguments for the decriminalisation of drug addiction and the treatment of addicts as suffering from a chronic condition. It is not so easy to convince the ordinary man in the street, who suffers from the addict's depredations, that this is a good idea. So far as he is concerned this will be just another example of taxpayers' money being doled out for the benefit of a self-indulgent minority who have brought the condition upon themselves. It is also the ordinary citizen who will have to live in close proximity to the addicts on such a support scheme and put up with any aberrant behaviour that might result.

There would always be a large number of people who would still buy drugs on the illicit market as they would not yet be fullblown addicts and not want to register. There would also be youngsters who might have difficulty in registering. A disincentive to registration might be the very strictly applied regulations and conditions necessary. Yet they are the very minimum essential for the organisation and running of a scheme with such a huge potential for abuse and corruption. The prohibitions imposed on registered addicts are, also, the very least necessary for the protection of the public. No government would dare to allow pilots or bus-drivers to continue their jobs if it was known that their judgement was faulty as a result of drugs. It is not just a matter of simply handing out drugs on demand. The liberalisation argument cannot be accepted at its face value; all of the most complex consequences must be considered. In any case, most of the liberalisers' alleged benefits would not materialise; the amount of money claimed to be saved by not sending addicts to jail would be more than equalled by the expense of running such a scheme satisfactorily.

8 Solutions

To the ordinary man in the street it seems that nothing can be done to curb the growth of drug addiction. Like a modern-day plague of biblical proportions, addiction visibly spreads and spreads, striking at the youngest and most vulnerable people in society. Yet, when the public look to their leaders for advice and action to stop the destructive flood of drugs, they receive little or no help, little action and only conflicting advice. It is not unreasonable to charge some politicians, the media, some members of the caring professions, and some churchmen, with gross dereliction of their duty to advise, inform, and act in time to have prevented the current drug situation from developing. People are bewildered by the pandemonium being caused now by the claims and counter claims being publicly aired by the same people whose failure to act, even ten years ago, has brought the country to its present state of near crisis. It should be remembered that it was failure to act in the past which has created the drug emergency that exists at present. Bewildered and concerned parents are being bombarded with leaflets and advice about the risks their children are being exposed to by the ever increasing availability of drugs. However, parents should not feel guilty about their own lack of knowledge. In fact they should feel angry at the impertinence of those who are, by implication, criticising their ignorance of drug abuse. Everyone has been the victim of the 'disinformation' propagandised for years.

Generally speaking, the arguments over the drug situation can be divided into three broad groups; those who think that the only answer is to educate young people not to take drugs, thus cutting the demand for them; those who think that the government should supply drugs to addicts free of charge, thus removing the drug barons' profits and stopping the illegal drug traffic; and those who think that the quickest, most effective and certain way is to prohibit drug abuse entirely and stop the production of drugs in the countries of origin by any means possible. Each of these ideas have supporters who argue for them in the hope of convincing the public that they are right, but many people are simply confused by the various claims.

The man in the street knows that after years of propaganda about the known dangers of smoking, young people are still smoking cigarettes. With drugs being even more addictive than cigarettes, it strikes him that simply telling youngsters why they should not use drugs will have no more effect than did telling them why they should not smoke tobacco. The idea that addicts should simply be supplied with free drugs also strikes ordinary people as strange. Drug addiction is seen by everyone as a bad and dangerous thing; why then, they wonder, would anyone want to make it a publicly funded activity. Most people feel that it would be good if the drug growers and manufacturers could be made to stop producing the drugs and sending them here, but they don't know how this might be done short of the use of armed force. Few men and women take seriously the suggestion that the Third World farmers who are growing the drugs should be paid to stop doing so; it seems too much like paying protection money to a criminal.

For most of a generation, during the 1960s and 1970s, some well known figures of the media, film and pop world, actively promoted the use of drugs. The civil liberties organisations were so busy defending people's rights that they failed to recognise the fact that addiction to drugs is a sentence to a life of misery from which there is no appeal. It may be that the people from the fleeting world of pop and show business are less guilty than more responsible members of society. Like the court jesters in past times, their living depends on the art of ingratiation, with the difference that they have to flatter and excite large numbers of people rather than a single monarch. They do not claim, usually, to be public spirited; in fact, many of them stress their self-interest in all things. When disaster struck medieval states, it was not the court jesters who were blamed, but the court. Similarly, the blame for the present drug problem cannot be placed on irresponsible pop singers and actors, but upon governments and social leaders who took no action then to counter the pro-drug message. Some may have feared to seem old fashioned; some may just not have recognised the drug dangers for the future. After all, intelligence and foresight have never been compulsory requirements for political office! Because of the obvious failure of the nation's leaders to appreciate or counter the dangers of the drug traffic in the past, pressure must come from the general public to produce effective and speedy measures to deal with the problem now and for the future. In order to do this effectively people need some background knowledge to give authority to their views.

It is vital that everyone should have some idea of possible ways of using parts of the three main suggestions for dealing with the drug problem; education to reduce demand; free supply to defeat the profit motive; and prevention of production by using various means to stop the whole drug traffic at source. This general knowledge will help people to weigh up the various proposals, to look critically at them, to decide how effective they might be, and decide how much they would cost and how long it would take the proposals to work. With the confidence of their own knowledge, people might then argue with the proposers of various schemes. Even more important, they might put pressure on the politicians for action and not risk being misled by soft words designed to deceive them into accepting inaction and no solutions.

9 Help for the addicted

There is a strong body of liberal opinion that argues against the policy of putting people in prison for possession of illegal drugs when the drugs are intended solely for personal use, not for dealing. It is claimed that, rather than helping the addict to get off drugs and return to a useful role in society, prison merely brings him into contact with criminals and gives him a course in crime. On his release he may use those lessons to obtain the money to support his drug addiction. It is suggested, therefore, that addicts should be treated as sick people suffering from a self-induced illness and, as such, they should be given treatment rather than imprisonment. They want government money to finance treatment centres for the cure of addiction in addition to extra funds for treatment within the health service.

The cost of keeping a man in prison in Britain can be as much as £375 per week and it is asserted that a treatment system would result in savings in public money, because treatment would be cheaper. Government would be expected to provide taxpayers' money to fund the addiction treatment centres, but it would not be given any role in their operation. On the face of it, this seems a sensible and economic way of dealing with the drug addicts; overcrowded prisons and overworked prison officers would be relieved of an unnecessary burden and public money would be saved. This is a much simplified version of the case put forward by the decriminalisation lobby, but it does contain the basic ideas and justification for the suggested change in the law.

It could be an excellent scheme if a number of conditions could be guaranteed; among them would have to be an assurance that it would work to the benefit of the addicts and to the country; that it would be safer and cheaper than sending addicts to jail; that it would bring an end to the drug trade, or at least abolish the market in drugs within the nation. Some of the criticisms of the scheme might include certain practical points. In effect, the scheme's proposers are assuming that all drug addicts will wish to be treated or will be content to be supplied with drugs from official sources as a form of drug maintenance. The evidence so far is that most addicts do not want treatment until they are in very serious trouble, and they tend to return to drug addiction as soon as they feel better.

The percentage of drug addicts who are apparently cured of their addiction is very low, as little as 3 per cent; the majority return to drugs. Even treatment with the drug methadone has not proved very successful. It was originally claimed that methadone could be substituted for heroin and that, by reducing the dose given over a period of time, the addict could be maintained at a level which would enable him either to function in society or to give up drugs altogether. Only about thirty per cent of addicts completed the three year treatment course, some became addicted to methadone, and many who were on the course were found to be taking illicit drugs in addition to their methadone.

It may be that most addicts cannot be cured by the usual voluntary means; perhaps the idea of a cure is one that should be attempted in a different way. The main drawback to treatment in voluntary centres is that the patients can walk out at any time and either buy drugs or just stay away altogether. A combination of treatment whilst in a secure environment, followed by residence in an open centre, might be more successful, as the addict would not have access to sources of illicit drugs, nor could he just walk out. Such a system of custodial treatment would probably find general public support.

CUSTODIAL TREATMENT AND REHABILITATION

Little change would be needed to amend the present laws on drug abuse to create a method of treatment capable of being operated for drug addicts within the present prison system. Psychiatric departments, borstals, and open prisons already exist within most prison departments and it would be quite an easy matter to create custodial drug treatment centres which would be operated and administered in the same way. They would, in effect, be special prisons, but would not carry the criminal stigma of the normal prisons; probably no more than – say – an alcoholic ward. Staff in these custodial centres would be specially trained in the skills needed to be prison officers with some medical knowledge to deal with prisoners who would also be patients.

The courts would have the option of a variety of custodial sentences when dealing with drug addicts, whether the offences committed were straightforward drug possession or crime carried out to buy drugs. This would be a rare instance of the law dealing with the actual motive for an offence, and not just the offence alone. Judges would be able to call on drug treatment specialists for advice on such matters as estimates of the prisoner's degree of addiction and the length of time needed to effect a possible cure. Sentences could then be adjusted for medical reasons, rather than according to any standard scale of imprisonment.

An addict sent to prison for a serious crime other than drug possession could be treated for his addiction until cured, then sent to an ordinary prison to complete his sentence. The ordinary addict jailed for possession of drugs would spend his whole sentence in the treatment centre, but a number of valuable options would be available which could be of benefit to him and to the taxpayer. If a cure was effected reasonably quickly, he could be sent to an open prison and early release could be a strong possibility. He could be allowed gradual access to the world outside the prison, and it would be quite easy to establish whether or not he was taking up drugs again as he would still be living in a supervised environment. If he was seen to be abstaining from drugs, he could be released on a conditional parole requiring him to stay in some post-treatment home for a given period. Provision could be made for the cancellation of parole and return to a treatment centre if he relapsed into drug abuse after release. This is only a very general outline of what would necessarily be a complex system to create, but it could be done, and it could be done quickly. Public opinion might be in favour of an idea which offers addicts the chance of cure and rehabilitation while serving their time in custody. Generally speaking the public are very sceptical about voluntary cures. They are after all the ones who suffer the thefts and trouble caused by the addicts in everyday life. It is certain that the cost of such a system would be only a fraction of the billions of dollars going to the drug barons annually from the drug infested countries.

10 Action against individual drug barons, their employees and organisations

The world's extradition laws are useless for dealing with the international nature of modern crime, especially drug trafficking. Extradition is, fundamentally, the surrender of an alleged criminal or convicted criminal by one state to another, but it is far from simple actually to achieve this. There is no internationally agreed procedure for guaranteeing that any criminal will be surrendered, even when the criminal is internationally notorious. The public have become accustomed to this fact by watching television programmes showing wanted criminals living lives of luxury on sun-drenched beaches all over the world. Whatever the legal hairsplitting may be that justifies this in the case of a robber, it is difficult to see how any justification can be made in the case of the drug barons and their employees. The governments of the drug producing countries hide behind the legal precedents that have built up over the years, and smugly do nothing in response to requests for the extradition of wanted drug traffickers. They outwardly pretend that they are unable to co-operate but they have no wish to do so.

It is because of the attitude of these corrupt governments that any hope of getting international agreement on the extradition of drug criminals is very unlikely, so the drug traders can enjoy their profits in the sun, with no fear of the law. It is because of this fact that some other means of bringing them to trial must be considered. There is precedent in the laws of England which was accepted internationally in the past, the piracy laws, and it may be possible to use them to deal with the old time pirate's modern equivalent – the international drug trafficker. Pirates traditionally boasted that they declared war on the whole world and they acted accordingly. The modern drug traders act in exactly the same way; they do not care who falls victim to their poison, be they foreigners or their own countrymen.

In English law, it was held that piracy was not a crime against any particular country but against all of mankind. Because this was so, it was accepted that any pirate could be tried and punished in any court, in any country wherever the pirate was found, or wherever he was taken for trial. It was accepted that anyone had the right to pursue and exterminate pirates anywhere, but it was not allowed for them to be killed without trial, except in battle. A further rule made it binding that any who surrendered were to be taken to a proper tribunal for trial. At the time the economies of all the world's trading nations were being damaged, to the point of disaster, by the depredations of the pirates on merchant ships. The deaths of honest seamen at that time were bitterly condemned. The similarities between the effects of piracy then and the effects of drugs now are remarkable. It would not be possible to get any international forum to promulgate an international law that would have the effect of the old piracy laws. The corrupt governments of the drug states would block and obstruct agreements for so long that they would, in effect, never become law. It would seem that the only way to tackle this would be for the countries most hard hit by drugs to agree among themselves that they would, in effect, treat drug offences across their frontiers as though they were offences of piracy. Between themselves, countries such as the EEC states, the USA, Australia, Canada and New Zealand, could agree that no extradition was needed for drug offenders; they would either return them for trial on request or, if more convenient, try them in their own courts.

This multilateral agreement would almost certainly be copied by other countries and could, before long, be effective in all civilized states. It might prove necessary to harmonise trial procedures, sentences, etc, between countries with different legal systems, but this would be a matter of administrative arrangement and could be dealt with quickly.

The initial aim would be to isolate the drug traffickers in their host countries; the ultimate aim would be for drug trafficking and its associated offences to be made criminal internationally by means of a truly international law. Such a law would have to be totally comprehensive and would need to apply to *all* drug offences, whether related to drugs made from plants or synthetic drugs or designer drugs. It would have to make it an internationally indictable offence to grow, manufacture, or traffic in any kind of drugs for illicit purposes anywhere. Trial, conviction and punishment would have to be allowable in any court of any country where the offender was found, or to which he might be taken. No trial would be permitted to be disallowed because of any claimed lack of jurisdiction. It would have to be accepted that, even if the offence occurred in some other country, because it was an offence against mankind, it could be tried anywhere. All nations would have to agree that if a drug offender was being traced, tracked or chased over national boundaries, there would be no need for the pursuers to obtain permission from the various states to continue with their duty. Whatever happens, and however it is done, there must be no safe place for the drug barons to sit in the sun.

11 Sanctions

People know through the media what nations are responsible for the flood of drugs pouring into their own country. Many are baffled and angry at their government's inability to persuade the governments of the drug states to stop the trade. It is felt that a major European power should be able to bring some pressure to bear on countries such as Bolivia, where the drug industry flourishes openly.

Generally speaking, no real pressure can be put on any of the drug states; they are protected by the collective security exemplified in the United Nations Organisation and can make accusations of interference in their national affairs at the slightest provocation. Drug smuggling on today's international scale was beyond imagining at the time of the creation of the UN, and so no rules of conduct or sanctions were drawn up to deal with such a situation. The underlying theme of the UN was the prevention of war and the improvement of the lot of all mankind. Unless some method of dealing with the drug producing states can be found which will bring a stop to drug production there could be, ironically, war as a result of some nation's patience running out. As disputes between individuals are better mediated or settled in a court rather than by fighting, it would seem that there is a need for a similar function to be carried out by the UN for the purpose of mediating between countries at odds because of drug trafficking. The UN will have to be given power to hear complaints about drug trafficking and be able to impose penalties or sanctions on any country which refuses to obey instructions to cease all such trade. Any sanctions imposed would have to be supported by all the member states in the UN on the clear understanding that drug abuse is against the interests of all mankind.

The past record of sanctions is not a good one and the sceptic can be excused for thinking that sanctions against the drug states would fare no better. However, political considerations, in which the great powers had a vested interest, were involved in all previous cases where sanctions were imposed. No such vested interest exists where drugs are concerned. Even if there were, no major power would wish to be held up before the whole world as the drug baron's friend. Relief and humanitarian aid and aid programmes would never be affected, for they are designed to assist the weakest and poorest people on earth. Such aid arises from feelings of sympathy for the plight of the poor and as a matter of simple humanity and morality. As the justification for imposing drug sanctions is basically a moral one, any harm done to those in need would be indefensible.

Every country in the modern world depends upon communications and the unhindered progress of ships, aircraft, motor traffic; trains, people, and goods. No country can survive without international trade and finance. Most of the countries engaged most heavily in the drug trade are in receipt of economic and technical aid, much of it provided by the very countries undergoing social disruption because of drugs. Any interruption of international trade and finance is immediately felt by the countries involved. The industrialised nations would be virtually unaffected by sanctions imposed on the drug producing states, as none of them provides any goods or raw materials which cannot be obtained elsewhere. Many of them, in fact, get better prices for their products than they otherwise would; agreements made with richer countries ensure them a market.

It is through the interlinking of the economies of all nations in today's world that pressure can be brought to bear on the drug producers. It is the men at the top who are profiting from drug money, not the man in the street, so it would only be fair to let the people know what is happening and why. Censorship is already imposed in countries such as Bolivia and Columbia, not so much by corrupt governments as by the drug barons. These men have already had newspapermen, judges, trade union leaders and politicians murdered merely for mildly criticising the drug trade. It would be necessary, therefore, to use every possible channel of modern communications and the media, to tell the ordinary people of any country that is about to have sanctions imposed against it, why it was being done, how it was intended to do it, and what would be necessary for the sanctions to be stopped – the end of drug production and export.

Churches, unions, women's organisations, and other groups would be asked to spread the information by word of mouth, and all would be asked to ensure that everyone knew that sanctions were coming because of the drug exports and not as a result of any other country's malice. It would be essential for them to know this because the corrupt leaders of the target country would be certain to try to play on the people's national pride. This would not be easy to do if every man, woman, and child knew that it was, in fact, because their country had been found guilty by the rest of the world of offending against humanity with their drugs.

Sanctions would have to be imposed gradually. The first step would probably be extended customs searches or document checks at borders, airports, and harbours, plus extended immigration procedures for all passengers from the country. The next step would probably be reduction of traffic through the international cable, satellite, telephone and telex networks; refusal of permission for the country's aircraft to pass through other countries' air space; refusal of letters of credit and trade guarantees. The next step would be to cut road, rail, air, river and shipping links. It is most unlikely that any of the countries concerned could sustain such pressure for long. Even their neighbours would refuse help because sanctions may be as easily applied to them as to the principal target.

Provision would have been made for dealing with sanctions' breakers. It is obvious that there will always be those who wish to make a financial or political profit out of sanctions, so it must be equally obvious that they must be stopped from doing so. It is almost certain that the ordinary people in the country under sanction would be the ones to force their government to change their ways, and they would be assisted in this by all the legitimate means available. Sanctions would be ended when the government of the drug producing country guaranteed to suppress the drug barons and UN forces would be made available to those governments too weak to combat the private armies employed by all the notorious drug barons. Most of the UN forces would probably be supplied to the UN from the coutnries most affected by drug smuggling and addiction.

It might be argued that sanctions are a very serious measure to apply against any sovereign state, as it is usually accepted that no interference is allowed in the internal affairs of any country. Under normal circumstances this would be so, but by growing, manufacturing and sending drugs into other countries, the drug states are interfering in those countries' internal affairs to a very marked degree.

By directing their drugs at other countries the drug states are doing great damage to them. Buildings may not be destroyed by drugs, but people are, and the overall consequences are just as bad – a battered economy and social ruin.

The electors in any democratic society may demand government action to stop the drug growers from producing drugs. In an election year some politicians could promise to do so, and could gain power with a mandate to take any necessary action against the guilty countries. In the nuclear age everyone is at risk if two nations become involved in war. It is very difficult to draw a line linking the junkie on the corner to global warfare, but it could happen. It is a possible scenario for what could happen and it is a very frightening one. Sanctions properly and firmly imposed could save the world from such a possibility.

12 International controls on chemicals used in drug manufacture

There are chemicals that are essential for the manufacture of drugs; without them the drug chemists could not manufacture heroin or cocaine, amphetamine or LSD, four of the most commonly abused drugs. Acetic anhydride is essential for the manufacture of heroin and cocaine. Ephedrine and phenyl-propanone are precursors used in the manufacture of amphetamine and LSD. Strict control of essential precursor chemicals would deal a mortal blow to the drug trade. These chemicals are much used in many legitimate manufacturing processes, mainly pharmaceutical, but their manufacture and sale, export and import could be monitored and controlled. It would be necessary for uniform legislation to be introduced into every country in the world community and it would require international recording, monitoring and inspection to ensure that the legislation was being obeyed to the letter. The number of manufacturers producing these chemicals globally is comparatively limited, and any workable control system would have to begin with them.

Lists of the chemicals required for drug manufacture should be compiled, and all manufacturers should be required to notify some central authority of every sale nationally or for export. Sales should only be permitted to companies that can prove legitimate need for these particular materials. When they are exported, certificates of export and receipt by the importer would be required, and could be cross-checked to ensure that the sale and the receiving company were genuine. Information about production, sale, export, and import of these chemicals could easily be recorded in national customs department computers linked to similar computers internationally. All the information would be held in common and any discrepancies or losses could be detected swiftly and appropriate action taken.

Such procedures may seem cumbersome but most transactions of this kind are, in any case, carried out by computer nowadays. Any reported losses in shipment or from stores would have to be carefully investigated and a record kept of the event. These recorded events could be monitored to establish whether or not there was a pattern that indicated organised theft, probably for drug manufacture. It might be possible to develop a tracer chemical which could be used to identify sources of manufacture, similar to the tracers put in oil to identify the origin of oil slicks. Legislation for this could be enacted fairly quickly, but until it is done, individual countries and groups of countries, such as the EEC, could initiate an informal system of control and monitoring. Certainly the computer technology exists which could make even an informal system effective until the introduction of a formal system. Any cost or complication arising from such a scheme can be as nothing compared to the harm being done by drugs.

13 Tracing and confiscating money and other assets

The sums of money made at various levels in the drug traffic are huge. The top drug barons are billionaires, the middlemen are millionaires, and even the small dealers are rich in any society. All these men are known because of their involvement in the drug trade and their vast wealth for which no legitimate source can be found. These men live outside the laws of all nations, except for the corrupt countries in which they live and do their business. They know that they are always at risk if they should fall into the hands of honest men, so they stay where they are safe. However, they could not carry on their trade without the use of banking and other financial institutions to keep and invest their fortunes. Because of the way drugs are sold on a cash-only basis, they have set up criminal organisations to 'launder' this money, that is, to disguise it to look as though it came from legitimate sources. Very large sums of money are involved, and sophisticated and complex techniques are used to disguise the source, ultimately these funds find their way into the legitimate banking and financial system. Although funds are transferred from country to country by devious means, most of the time they are passed through normal money routes also. Banking secrecy, designed to protect the private financial affairs of honest men, also protects the secrets of drug criminals.

It can be understood why bankers will not voluntarily offer information about the private finances of their customers. No banker would stay in business for very long if he gained a reputation for being loose-mouthed about his clients. In Switzerland the banking secrecy laws are so strict that an incautious banker can be sent to prison for breach of confidentiality. Police and customs officers are constantly obstructed by perfectly legitimate refusals to reveal financial information. No doubt the respectable businessmen who act in this manner would be horrified to be thought of as aiders and abetters of the drug trade. Governments have to devise ways of detecting, identifying and seizing this money and any other assets made from the trade in drugs. This will not be too easy, as the professionals who are engaged in the laundering of the money are highly paid, highly skilled, and very knowledgeable. They are experts in the field of international finance and have legitimate contacts in the money markets of the world. From Hong Kong to Switzerland and Panama they know all the banking rules; which banks have the best secrecy record, and who will move very large amounts of money with no embarrassing questions asked. Governments will have to employ men and methods capable of dealing with these men and these methods.

The money is more easily detected in the early stages when it has only recently come from the streets. Bankers and other money men know perfectly well that few companies are making very big profits in business just now; fewer still are making profits for little or no outlay of money. Any experienced banker will become suspicious if he sees regular and large amounts coming into his branch for no detectable business done. It is essential that some means are devised by which such suspicions can be brought to the attention of the authorities without the banker's involvement becoming known. Even more odd is the constant payment, in small denomination notes, of large amounts of money, or the regular changing of small denomination bank notes for bills of larger denominations.

It is possible that monitoring of large financial movements between different countries may give the authorities a better chance of detecting unusual transfers of money for which no obvious source can be found. The greatest weapon against the drug money men may be the computer. All money movements out of the country, other than cash smuggled out, shows up in the currency movements displayed by financial computers. A computer can be programmed to detect any anomalies, that is, any movement of large sums of money for which no previous transaction was indicated. It would be rather like seeing a ripple going across a pond without seeing the fish making it. The objective of the police would then be to find out where the money came from, and where it was going to.

The Treasury monitors all the movements of money within the

UK, for example, and that which is coming in and going out from the great financial institutions in London. Although Treasury officers are mainly interested in very large movements which affect the general economy, they also may observe anomalies; if so, these must be investigated. The monitoring computer could as easily be programmed to look for sums that are involved in large cash transactions above a certain amount and indicate them for investigation.

Bank secrecy laws must be changed. Banker's suspicions must be translated into action. The drug money must be detected and seized. Any assets bought with drug money must be 'frozen' and later action must be taken to confiscate those assets. The reason for all this is not just to put money into the Treasury, it is to hurt the drug traffickers.

Money is the drug baron's main weapon in his armoury of corruption; without it he is out of business. There is no loyalty in the drug world, only money. Some drug barons have private armies of hundreds of men, all of them well armed and prepared to kill. They will be loyal to him so long as he pays, in cash. He can corrupt, and kill, and buy governments, and kill judges, with impunity. By corrupting just one man in an organisation, such as police or customs, he may bring to naught all the efforts of a country trying to curb the sales of drug to young people. If the supply of money dries up, then the supply of drugs will dry up.

Once the laundered money is detected, the police can do more than just arrange for it to be confiscated, they can trace it back to its sources and find out who was involved in the criminal laundering operation. Just as important would be any clues that could lead them to the drug transaction agents, the men who set up drug deals between the drug barons and the dealers who act as wholesalers in the UK as part of the drug distribution network. Even suspicion of involvement with drug money could be enough to give the police a hint worth further investigation. Money is the reason for the drug trade; interrupt its flow and the flow of drugs is interrupted all down the line.

This cannot be done cheaply. Highly qualified and skilled men will have to be employed at salaries commensurate with their skills. Computers, which are compatible with similar computers used by police and customs in other countries, will be needed to combat the drug trade with high technology. Total liaison will be essential between the law enforcement officers of the nation and their colleagues overseas. Training, equipment, men and women, aircraft, vessels, vehicles – they are all expensive, but not as expensive as the yearly cost of drugs. Once politicians realise that the people want this done, and done quickly, action will be taken but the people need to know what is required, and why.

PART IV
The Drugs and their Effects

14 Narcotics

Heroin

Slang names: smack; scag; horse; stuff; joy powder; Harry boy
It is plant-derived from the opium poppy. It is usually sold as a powder although it is also sold in the form of red pills in the Far East. In colour, the powder may range from white to fawn, white being the purest (89 to 99 per cent). It is common for the purity to be diluted at each stage of sale from the wholesaler to the street-dealer; any white powder may be used to 'cut' the purity to increase the profit for the dealer, eg, lactose, talcum powder, quinine, chalk dust, scouring powder and fine sugar. Heroin is commonly cut to as little as thirty per cent purity for smoking but may in some cases be cut to as low as seven per cent.

Methods of use

It is usually smoked or injected with an average consumption of 9–12mg per day.

Smoking
'Chasing the dragon' The heroin is heated on a piece of tinfoil and the fumes inhaled through a tube.

'Playing the mouth organ' The heroin is heated on a tinfoil and the smoke drawn in and inhaled through the rectangular cover of a matchbox.

'Firing the anti-aircraft gun' A small quantity of heroin is placed on the tip of a cigarette which is smoked tilted upwards.

Mainlining The heroin is placed in a syringe, dissolved in water or blood, and injected into a vein. Usually blood is drawn up into the syringe to ensure a good mix. Heroin is rarely sniffed, and very rarely swallowed as the digestive system dilutes the effects.

Heroin pills (known as Hoong Yoon) are rarely seen in western countries, being mainly limited to Oriental heroin smokers.

Subjective effects of taking heroin

Usual duration of effect from 3 to 6hr. Heroin acts as a block to physical pain and undesired mental states. It produces a sense of euphoria or wellbeing which makes pain, anxiety or depression seem unimportant. It has been described as giving an orgasmlike rush or flash that lasts briefly but memorably. At the peak of the euphoria, the user has a feeling of exaggerated physical and mental comfort and wellbeing; a heightened feeling of buoyancy and bodily health, and a heightened feeling of being competent, in control, capable of any achievement, and being able to cope.

Possible true effects upon the user

Euphoria (a sense of wellbeing); drowsiness; respiratory depression; constricted pupils of the eyes, and nausea.

Effects of an overdose

It is rare for an addict to overdose as a result of smoking heroin; this normally results from injection (mainlining) with heroin which is either much purer than the user is accustomed to, or of too large a quantity. The signs of overdose are slow and shallow breathing, clammy skin, convulsions, coma, and possible death. The possibility of death is heightened if the addict has been mixing heroin with any other drug or with alcohol. He may suffocate by choking on his own vomit whilst unconscious.

Effects of withdrawal

Heroin is a highly addictive drug whose effects upon a regular user are to create a higher physical and psychological dependence. Thus, when a heroin addict is deprived of his drug, or stops using it, he experiences unpleasant physical and psychological effects. These are commonly: watery eyes; runny nose; loss of appetite; yawning; irritability; tremors; panic; chills and sweating; severe cramps, and nausea. Whilst very unpleasant, withdrawal symptoms do not usually result in death in the absence of any other medical condition.

Long term effects of narcotic abuse

There are a number of dangerous and even potentially fatal effects which may result from narcotics' abuse. Anorexia, malnutrition and anaemia are common conditions for addicts. Resistance to infection is greatly reduced. The old killer disease, tuberculosis, almost abolished by penicillin and other antibiotics, may be contracted by addicts as a consequence of their debilitation. The practice of communal injection sessions, with addicts sharing unsterile needles and syringes, can result in abscesses, cellulitis, and severe infection. Aids is also spread by communal needles and syringes.

By constantly injecting into the same veins, addicts cause the walls of the veins to lose their elasticity and to collapse. When this happens addicts will move on to other veins, sometimes in the toes and feet. Eventually they may use the veins in the groin, and this frequently results in the creation of blood clots which cause gangrene and inevitable amputations.

Bacteria and viruses may get into the bloodstream through dirty or shared needles and can cause inflamation of the heart valves and heart lining (endocarditis), tetanus which may prove fatal, and hepatitis.

Impurities and adulterants used by dealers to 'cut' the drug may cause kidney failure; substances such as flour may have serious effects, such as blood clotting. The risk of death, and very unpleasant death too, is always an option of a 'fix'.

OPIUM

Brand names: Dovers Powder; Paregoric; J. Collis Browne's Mixture; Parepectolin

Medical use: analgesic (pain reliever) and anti-diarrhoeal. It has a high physical and psychological dependence.

Methods of use: oral or smoked.

Effects: as for heroin.

MORPHINE

Brand names: Morphine and Pectoral Syrup.

Medical use: analgesic and antitussive (stops coughing). It has a high physical and psychological dependence.
Methods of use: oral and injected.
Effects: as for heroin.

CODEINE

Brand names: Tylenol with codeine; Empirin compound with codeine; Robitussan; Codis
Medical use: analgesic, antitussive. It has a moderate physical and psychological dependence.
Methods of use: oral or injected.
Effects: as for heroin.

HYDROMORPHONE

Brand names: Dilaudid.
Medical use: analgesic. It has a high physical and psychological dependence.
Methods of use: oral or injected.
Effects: as for heroin.

PETHIDINE (also known as meperidine)

Brand names: Demerol; Mepergan.
Medical use: analgesic. It has a high physical and psychological dependence.
Methods of use: oral or injected.
Effects: as for heroin.

METHADONE

Brand names: Dolophine; Methadone; Physeptone; Methadose.
Medical use: analgesic. It has a high physical, but low psychological dependence.
Methods of use: oral or injected.
Effects: as for heroin, lasting from 12 to 24hr, compared to the other drugs above which commonly last from 3 to 6hr.

Methadone is being used in drug treatment for detoxifying

addicts, but evidence is demonstrating that less than one in three completes the treatment and many others become strongly addicted to the methadone itself.

OTHERS

Brand names: Lomotil; Fentanyl; Darvon; Numorphan; LAAM; Leritine; Tussionex; Percodan; Talwin.
Medical use: anti-diarrhoeal; analgesic; antitussive. All have low physical and psychological dependence.
Methods of use: oral or injected.
Effects: as above, with variable duration. Some have unpleasant side effects eg, overuse of Lomotil can cause blindness.

15 Stimulants

COCAINE

Slang names: coke; snow; angel dust; Charlie; flake
This is plant-derived from the coca bush and is usually sold as a white bitter-tasting crystalline powder. It may be diluted by the addition of adulterants – 'cutting'.

Methods of use

It may be sniffed, smoked or injected, but the most common method is sniffing up through a straw or a rolled up bank note – known as 'snorting'. Generally the cocaine is lined up on a smooth surface, such as a handbag mirror, in a line about one inch long by an eighth of an inch wide containing from to 25 to 30mg of the drug, then sniffed up into the nostrils with sharp inhalations – hence 'snorting.' It may be injected into a vein or just under the skin, or it may be added in small quantities to a cigarette and smoked.

Subjective effects of taking cocaine

Usual duration of effect between 1 and 2hr. Cocaine has a very strong stimulant effect which is commonly felt within three minutes of taking the drug. The user feels strong, self-confident, exhilarated and in charge. Feelings of fatigue, hunger and self-doubt disappear. It is claimed by some that use of cocaine heightens or restores their flagging virility, and enables them to extend the sex act for long periods. It is also claimed by some that the effect is like a long-extended orgasm.

Possible true effects upon the user

Increased alertness; excitation; euphoria; increased pulse rate and blood pressure; insomnia, and possible severe loss of appetite. Regular use may result in: damage to the nasal membranes; an anorexic condition; habitual sniffing; nose-pulling; picking; plucking, or squeezing. Regular users may become prey to a persecution complex or paranoia.

Effects of an overdose

The user who has overdosed may display extreme agitation; an increase in body temperature; experience hallucinations, some of which may result in extreme or violent behaviour; violent convulsions through the spinal cord; depression of the nervous system and death.

Effects of withdrawal

Although physical dependence on cocaine is rated as only low to medium, possible psychological dependence is high in addicts. The addict undergoes an irresistible compulsion to use the drug in increasing dosages and at ever-increasing frequencies, regardless of physical, pyschological and personal consequences. The withdrawal syndrome is characterised by apathy, long periods of sleep, extreme fatigue, irritability, depression and disorientation. These effects are worth noting when it is known that the cocaine high may last only 30min and the addict user will then need another 'snort' or have to face the consequences.

CRACK (ROCK) (freebase cocaine)

Crack or rock is obtained from cocaine by separation of the adulterants from the cocaine by mixing it with water and ammonium hydroxide. The water is then removed from the cocaine base by means of a fast drying solvent, either being the most commonly used. The resultant mixture resembles large sugar crystals, similar to rock sugar. This is a highly addictive form of cocaine, and some US authorities claim that one use is enough to cause addiction. An additional incentive to use is the claim that it is difficult to debase or to cut crack without it becoming obvious to the addict.

Method of use

It is usually smoked, either in a specially made glass pipe, or mixed in with tobacco, or with marijuana in a cigarette. Crack is so much more addictive than cocaine, that users commonly admit that immediately they have finished one dose they crave another.

Subjective effects of taking crack (rock)

Usual duration of effect – fleeting. Similar to the effects of standard cocaine but, according to users, the 'rush' is more immediate, gives a greater 'high' and has an even greater orgasmic effect, but this is immediately followed by an insistent desire to have another fix.

Possible true effects upon the user

Increased alertness to the extent of hyper-alertness; excitation; euphoria; increased pulse rate; increased blood pressure; insomnia; loss of appetite; and, as 'crack' is even more addictive than powdered cocaine, the craving for more exists almost immediately after a 'fix'.

Effects of an overdose

Overdoses are more common when drugs are injected than when they are smoked; however, because of the immediate and irresistible compulsion for more crack, the effects of an overdose could be as for cocaine – agitation; increase in body temperature; hallucination; convulsions; possible death.

Effects of withdrawal

Intense craving for the drug amounts to an irresistible compulsion to have it, but the only possible cure for cocaine (crack) addiction is complete abstinence from the drug. Withdrawal is characterised by apathy, long periods of sleep, extreme fatigue, irritability, depression, and disorientation.

Long term effects of cocaine use

Because of the cocaine's anaesthetic effect, cocaine crystals, and the sometimes very abrasive adulterants used by dealers to 'cut' the drug, can abrade the tissues lining the nose without the user realising it. The constrictive effect of the drug on the blood vessels in the nose can stop the flow of blood to an area of injury, and the mucous membrane may not be restored. Heavy dosages of cocaine taken over a long period can make a permanent hole in the cartilage that separates the nostrils.

As with the injection of all drugs, the users are subject to abscesses, cellulitis and infections. Dirty, unsterile needles and syringes can cause Aids, hepatitis or potentially fatal tetanus or inflamation of the membranes around the heart. Adulterants and impurities used by dealers to 'cut' the cocaine can cause serious damage to the kidneys, and some substances, such as flour, may lead to clotting of the blood. There is always the risk of an air bubble or embolism being injected with serious (often fatal) consequences.

Communal use of needles, syringes and other paraphernalia, spreads Aids. Cocaine can have serious effects on the heart, straining it with high blood pressure, with interrupted heart rhythm, and with raised pulse rates. The liver may also be damaged. Severe convulsions can cause incurable brain damage and sometimes death. The psychosis caused by cocaine use may lead to a lifetime of mental and emotional problems. In addition to any or all of these effects, 'crack' smokers may also suffer lung damage. Any use of cocaine can lead to death.

AMPHETAMINES

Slang names: speed; whizz
Brand names: Dexedrine; Biphetamine; Delcobese; Desoxyn; Mediatric

Medical use

Sleeping sickness; weight control. These are commercially manufactured drugs. Amphetamines are the most widely abused of the stimulant drugs in the UK because of the ease with which they may be obtained by prescription and by purchase, or by theft of prescribed pills within the family. Amphetamines come in the form of pills or capsules or as a white or a brown powder. When powdered they may be adulterated or 'cut'.

Methods of use

They may be sniffed, swallowed or injected. Both the powder form and pills reduced to a powder may be injected into a vein or immediately under the skin.

Subjective effects of taking amphetamines

Usual duration of effect, from 2 to 4hr. Users experience a strong stimulant effect; a 'rush' or 'high'. They feel alert, energetic, and confident. Any feelings of fatigue, hunger and self-doubt disappear.

Possible true effects upon the user

Habitual or prolonged use may be evidenced by hyper-alertness; excitation; euphoria; increased pulse rate and blood pressure; insomnia; loss of appetite.

These users may become thin and haggard as they are burning up energy at an abnormal rate whilst eating badly and that only occasionally. Their appearance may be further marked by lack of sleep. Prolonged use can lead to irritability, deep anxiety feelings, and an irrational persectution complex that can lead to sudden acts of violence, even to murder. Communal injection sessions may expose the addicts to Aids, hepatitis, and other diseases.

Effects of an overdose

An overdose is more likely when the drug is injected than when it is swallowed or sniffed. The maximum safe dose in one day is 30mg. An overdose may be characterised by agitation; increase in body temperature; hallucinations; severe convulsions; and possible death. Medical help is urgently required in case of an overdose, amateur attempts at first aid could prove fatal.

Effects of withdrawal

Although there is little evidence for physical dependence on amphetamines, there is a high degree of psychological dependence. Withdrawal is characterised by apathy, by long periods of deep sleep, irritability, exhaustion, and by severe depression and disorientation.

Long term effects of abuse of amphetamines and other stimulants

Long term abuse of amphetamines and similar stimulants can lead to very severe effects. Great strain is put on the cardiovascular system; this may lead to high blood pressure and irregular heart rhythm, and the possibility of a stroke. The retinas can be damaged as a result of injuries caused to the blood vessels supplying the eyes.

Users experience loss of appetite to the degree that they become malnourished. This, together with drug-induced sleeplessness, lowers the user's resistance to disease and infections and leads to a variety of illnesses.

Users who inject the drug are prey to all the usual problems of infections at the site of injections, blood-poisoning, hepatitis, inflammation of the membrane of the heart and, if sharing needles and syringes, Aids.

Large doses of methylamphetamine may lead to the rupture of small blood vessels supplying the brain, and may cause permanent damage to the brain. The ease with which these drugs may be obtained by almost anyone, sometimes on prescription, makes them exceedingly dangerous.

OTHERS

Cocaine, crack and amphetamines are only three of the stimulant drugs which are subject to illicit use. Some others are: Phenmetrazine (Preludrin); Adipex; Bacarate; Cylert; Didrex; Ionamin; Plegine; Pre-Sate; Sanorex; Tenuate; Tepanil; and Voranil. When misused, these drugs are reportedly similar to amphetamines in all respects. They are manufactured for legitimate use in hyperkinesis, narcolepsy, and in weight control.

16 Depressants

BARBITURATES

Slang names: barbies; downers
Brand names: seconal; Amytal; Tuinal; Nembutal; Soneryl; Luminal

Medical use

Sedation; relief from anxiety; anti-convulsant; also a hypnotic used for anaesthesia.

These are commercially manufactured for legitimate use in the form of white crystalline powder supplied in pills and capsules.

Methods of use

It is usually taken orally or injected and is frequently used in conjunction with alcohol to amplify its effects.

Subjective effects

Usual duration of effect from 1 to 16hr. Initially, similar to strong alcohol. Users experience relief from ihibitions, have a feeling of jovial good humour and euphoria; they feel 'high' and are passively content. These moods can change rapidly to gloom, agitation and belligerent violence.

True effects upon the user

Slurred speech; disorientation; staggering; appearance of confusion; may become aggressive and violent because of the befuddlement. A user may take more of the drug or mix it with another drug or with an excess of alcohol and go into a coma or die.

Effects of an overdose

In the confusion caused by abuse, overdoses are common either because the user takes too much, or because he combines two or more drugs, or he mixes the drug with alcohol. Characteristic signs of overdose include a clammy skin; dilated pupils; weak and rapid pulse; shallow respiration which may lead to coma and death. Professional medical attention is urgently needed for anyone in this condition.

Effects of withdrawal

Barbiturates are highly addictive and withdrawal effects are severe, characterised by anxiety; insomnia; dizziness; tremors; twitching; nausea; seizures; distorted eye-sight; convulsions, and possible death. Professional medical attention is urgently required for anyone in this condition. The barbiturates are not the only prescription drugs that are commonly abused.

BENZODIAZEPINES

Brand names: Valium; Librium; Diazepam; Ativan; Seranid; Dalmene; Halcion; Mogadon

Medical use

Anti-anxiety, anti-convulsant, sedative and hypnotic. Although low in potential for physical and psychological dependence when used medically, the dependence risk increases when used in high doses for a prolonged period. A further danger arises from their increasing use in multiple drug abuse (polyabuse).

Methods of use

Oral or injected.

Effects

Generally as for Barbiturates lasting for 4 to 8hr.

CHLORAL HYDRATE

Brand names: Notec; Chloral Elixir or Mixture

Medical use
Sedation; for insomnia. There is moderate potential for physical and psychological dependence.

Method of use
Oral.

Effects
As for barbiturates, lasting from 5 to 8hr. Not, now, a common drug of abuse.

CHLORMETHIAZOLE

Brand names: Heminevrin

Medical use
Sedative for the elderly; for acute withdrawal symptoms in the treatment of alcoholics.

Methods of use
Oral or injected.

Effects
As for barbiturates, lasting 4hr. Withdrawal may be extremely serious and medical treatment should be urgently sought.

MEPROBAMATE

Brand names: Equanil; Meprate; Tenavoid

Medical use
Anti-anxiety especially when accompanied by muscle spasms; sedative; hypnotic. Moderate potential for physical and psychological dependence.

Method of use

Oral or injected.

Effects

As for barbiturates, lasting from 4 to 8hr. Has only moderate potential for abuse.

Long term effects of depressants

There are so many of these drugs about, both legitimately and illicitly, that prolonged use is comparatively easy with regard to supply and price. All the adverse effects described above may be experienced over a prolonged period and range from minor accidents to death. The liver may be damaged, to the extent that nerve damage may occur, with severe effects upon the victim. Malnutrition is common, with all the attendant risks of inability to fight infections and disease. For those who inject, there are all the usual needle and syringe diseases: hepatitis; cellulitis; abscesses; inflammation of the heart membrane; Aids, etc. Lack of balance or lack of muscle control or inability to judge speeds and distances, etc, can all lead to simple, everyday activities such as driving a car, or mowing the lawn, or even crossing the street, becoming lethal exercises.

17 Hallucinogens

There are approximately twenty or more plant-derived and synthetic hallucinogens in existence, few of which have any known, legitimate medical use. One other (phencyclidine) can be used as a veterinary anaesthetic. All hallucinogens are dangerous; even in medical treatment they are used with extreme caution.

LSD (D-lysergic acid diethylamide)

Slang names: acid; microdot

LSD is a synthetic and one of the most potent psychoactive drugs, which is obtained from the fungus ergot, that grows on rye and some sunflowers. It is commonly known as 'rust'.

Method of use

Oral. It is sold as small spots on small pieces of blotting paper (blotter acid); as coloured tablets about the size of an aspirin (tab acid); as tiny pinhead-sized tablets (micro-dots); and may also be supplied in small impregnated squares of paper (stamps).

Subjective effects

Generally the effects felt are related to the quantity of LSD taken. A low dose (10 to 25mcg – micrograms are millionths of a gram), will produce mild euphoria and loss of inhibitions. If a higher dose is taken (50 to 100mcg and up to 400 to 500mcg), psychedelic effects are experienced. Usually sensory perceptions are heightened, shapes look sharper and more clearly defined, tastes seem tastier, and sounds seem purer and louder. The senses may interchange so that the user hears colour, or sees sound, or tastes with touch. Users may see after-images of movement like the trails sometimes seen on a TV screen; psychedelic patterns and streaks of colour may be seen. Strange body sensations may be felt such as floating or heaviness. Users become highly suggestible and easily manipulated; seduction of males and females alike becomes easier.

The hallucinations are most often visual, but users are generally aware that they are unreal. There is a great sense of detachment which may terrify some users. Perceptions of time and distance are poor. Adverse reactions may also be experienced, and are dealt with below. Duration of effects is between 8 and 12hr.

Possible true effects

The physiological effects of taking LSD are experienced in the body's response to the drug's impact on the central nervous system. They seem less related to the quantity of the drug taken than do the psychological effects. The symptoms are a rising temperature and blood pressure, enlarged pupils and rapid heart beat. Sweating may alternate with shivering, appetite is lost and nausea felt and all this may be accompanied by fear and agitation, and by insomnia. As the effects wear off, the user may be left feeling tense, nervous, highly strung and washed out.

Some users may experience a totally 'bad trip' where effects may be felt which range from anxiety and panic to complete psychosis and where the sense of personal identity is lost. Mental confusion and befuddlement are felt. Delusions of all types occur. Paronoia and hallucinations are accepted as reality. Panic reactions may, at times, last for more than 48 hours. Skilled medical and psychiatric help may be necessary for users experiencing these effects.

Effects of an overdose

It is commonly accepted that even a massive overdose of LSD will not prove fatal, as the drug does not damage the body's organs. The major threat to the life of the user and others lies in the psychotic reactions brought about by drug-behavioural toxicity. Extreme psychotic reactions may occur during use, and for intermittent periods long after use has stopped. These occurrences are called 'flashbacks'. Deep depression may be felt, leading to suicide. But, potentially more life threatening, is the involuntary re-experience of the hallucinations, which may occur once, or frequently, over a period of months. The cause of 'flashbacks' is not known. Although, they may occur when the user is under stress, or drinking alcohol, or using another drug such as cannabis. They are just as likely to occur without any apparent cause. The flashbacks may last for hours and happen at any time and place, with no advance warning. It is the sudden, unexpected onset which is the major threat to life. A user could be driving a car, or a train, or flying an aircraft, or running a nuclear power station when a flashback occurs, and many innocent people could be injured or killed as a result. There would be no obvious post mortem evidence in the user's body to show why. Some individuals, who have experienced flashback delusions and hallucinations long after using LSD, have died as a result of attempting to fly from high buildings, or have tried to stop oncoming vehicles by the exercise of their willpower.

Withdrawal symptoms

There is no evidence of physical or psychological dependence on LSD by users. They develop tolerance to the drug very rapidly to such an extent that the effects they expect cannot be achieved without larger doses. Cessation of use, for even a few days, will restore the user's sensitivity to the drug, enabling him to take smaller quantities.

LSA (D-lysergic acid amide)

LSA is derived from 'Morning Glory' seeds. It is usually no more than 10 per cent the strength of LSD. Among the unpleasant side-effects are nausea and diarrhoea. Other effects are similar to LSD, they may last 8 to 12hr, and may cause flashback symptoms.

DMT, DET AND DPT

These are chemically related and give quickly felt effects. The effects of DMT may be felt for up to 45min. DET and DPT effects may last from 2 to 6hr. It is usually smoked (commonly with cannabis), but can also be injected. The effects are similar to those of LSD, but stronger, more intense are felt quicker and end sooner. Among users, DMT is known as the 'businessman's high' as it can be used and experienced quickly. However, all the disadvantages of LSD may be felt with DMT, DET and DPT.

MAGIC MUSHROOMS

Psilocybin and psilocin are found in approximately ninety species of mushrooms that grow naturally in Europe. Psilocybin is changed in the body of the consumer into psilocin which is more potent in its effects. Although, only one-hundredth the strength of a dose of LSD, the effects are similar. The effects of eating up to 10gm of the dried mushrooms may last from 4 to 6hr. Possession and use of these mushrooms is not, as yet, an offence in the UK and the gathering of these halluncinogenic fungi has become something of a cult activity. The dangers are similar to those of LSD.

MESCALINE

Slang names: mesc, buttons, cactus
It is a plant-derived drug from the peyote cactus.

Method of use
Oral, in 200mg doses (milligrams are thousandths of a gram). Sold as buttons of up to 40mg.

Subjective effects
The effects are similar to those of LSD, lasting from 8 to 12hr.

True effects
Nausea and vomiting are frequently experienced. Physical effects can be extremely severe if high doses are consumed. The toxicity of the drugs can seriously affect the digestive system. A 'bad trip' may be life threatening.

Effects of an overdose
Although overdoses are unusual (mescaline is in short supply), they may occur, causing death. Urgent medical attention is needed for an overdose case.

Withdrawal symptoms
Mescaline does not appear to create physical or psychological dependence and no withdrawal symptoms have been recorded.

DOM

It is a hallucinogenic amphetamine variant. It has also been named STP, after the fuel oil additive.

Method of use

Oral or injected.

Effects

Produces LSD-type effects at doses up to 5mg which may last as long as 24hr. This is a very dangerous drug, characterised by frequent 'bad trips'. Drug-induced psychosis may affect the user for many years, and overdoses are very likely to be fatal.

DOB

This is a derivative of DOM. Although only 10 per cent of the strength of LSD, it may be sold to users as LSD, exposing them to the extreme dangers associated with DOM.

MDA AND MDM

Slang names: XTC – ecstacy, Love drug
MDM is a new drug similar to MDA in all respects. Although they are hallucinogens, their effects differ considerably from those of LSD. If anything, they may be more dangerous in their appeal to the shy, the lonely, the young and insecure. At doses of up to 150mg, they reportedly give the user feelings of serenity, calm and euphoria, and encourage feelings and acts of affection. These drugs' effects change rapidly at dosages in excess of 150mg with the user perspiring, becoming prey to tension and experiencing hallucinations whose vagueness, or lack of clarity, may increase feelings of fear. In addition to all other hallucinatory effects, MDA and MDM users seem to develop the desire for further doses. These drugs have a marked potential for abuse and users may become addicted to them. Consumption of doses in excess of 200mg may cause death. The principal danger with these drugs is the connotation, in the minds or potential users, caused by the terms 'ecstacy' and 'love' drugs. This may encourage them to ignore the horrors caused by what might only be a few milligrams under a lethal dose.

PHENCYCLIDINE

Slang names: angel dust; hog; PCP

A dangerous, chemically derived drug. Most commonly supplied as powder or liquid and only rarely in tablet form, and sold cheaply.

Methods of use

Oral, sniffed, injected, or sprayed, dusted or mixed with marijuana and smoked. A dose as low as 5mg will produce hallucination.

Subjective effects

PCP may seem like a high-powered, potent cannabis in dosages up to 5mg. Larger dosages produce effects which are totally unpredictable. Users experience LSD-type hallucinations, visual distortions, and illusions, often accompanied by strange bodily sensations, such as immunity from pain or the feeling of being made of rubber. Paralysis may also occur for varying periods of time.

True effects

The effects of this very potent drug can be extraordinarily severe and its rapid spread can only be explained by its cheapness, since the physical and mental dangers are horrendous! The margin of risk is a knife edge between a dose of PCP that gives the desired effect, and a catalogue of severely adverse reactions. Among the lesser traumas are extreme nausea, vomiting, severe cramps, agitation, depression and a feeling of paranoia. Temporary paralysis is also present. More severe results may include high blood pressure; increased heart rate; rapid eye movements; sweating; drooling; and the discharge of mucous from the nose. Users may exhibit extreme agitation and may become very violent.

Persons in this condition need qualified medical help urgently, they are extremely dangerous and may injure themselves and others, possibly fatally.

Effects of an overdose

The margin between tolerable doses and toxic doses is so fine that it can vary between individuals to such an extent that it can be bewildering. It is as well to acknowledge that any dose might result in an overdose, even the first. Death may come in many guises as a result of the varied adverse reactions. PCP users have drowned on numerous occasions while bathing, or swimming, in an attempt to cool their hot dry skins. This discomfort comes about because of raised body temperatures. The search for water can become obsessive.

The anaesthetic effect of the drug can give an insensitivity to pain that leads to accidents and self-inflicted injuries. Users can experience paranoid delusions and become violently aggressive.

Those who indulge in heavy dosages show long-lasting mental impairment; memory lapses; some disorientation and befuddlement; speech impairment; and sight problems with disturbance of vision. All these problems may last for a year or longer. Some may suffer very, very high blood pressure; prolonged coma; severe convulsions; and death. An overdose victim may become catatonic and lie rigid, in a state like living-death. Violent behaviour may last for days, normal behaviour returns only after several weeks. Psychosis may last for very long periods, and it is possible that permanent brain damage can occur from which the victim never recovers. Even hospital treatment may not be sufficient to help, other than by administering heavy sedation; death can still occur.

Withdrawal symptoms

It is not yet certain whether or not physical dependence on PCP may develop. It is definite that psychological dependence is created, and users will display symptoms of withdrawal. PCP users do tend to increase their dosages. Like THC (see cannabis below), PCP is absorbed into the fatty tissues of the body and is only released gradually, so a further dose adds to the residue still in the body to produce an overdose.

It must be repeated that this is a very dangerous drug, made more dangerous by the fact that it could be taken inadvertently by someone who thought he was just smoking cannabis. PCP has been known to have been sprayed on cannabis.

All hallucinogens are dangerous to both users and innocent bystanders, as the effects of their use are so unpredictable. The greatest danger for the innocent lies in the flashbacks so commonly experienced, even long after use has ceased. It may be that the answer to many unexplained disasters lies in the unknown indulgence of an individual in some *later undetectable* hallucinogenic substance.

18 Cannabinoids

CANNABIS

Slang names: grass, pot, tea, Mary Jane, wacky backy, dope, reefer, ghangha, black, gold (with the name of the country of origin), and marijuana

It is derived from the hemp plant (*Cannabis sativa*). Usually it is sold as a herbal mixture made from the leaves, twigs, seeds, and flower tops.

Method of use

Usually smoked as a hand-rolled cigarette or in a pipe. The marijuana may at times be mixed with tobacco. May also be taken by mouth, in food such as hash biscuits or fudge.

Subjective effects

Cannabis has sedative properties and creates in the user a sense of relaxed wellbeing, and freedom from inhibition. There may also be mild hallucinations that create a dreamy state in which the user may experience fantasies. Smokers become highly suggestible and may agree to, or engage in, actions and activities, especially sexual, in which they would not be involved under normal circumstances. Perceptions of distance, dimensions, and of time may be distorted. Smokers may take the drug to improve their social performance, but generally this is user-subjective since an increased consumption will slow down thought and responses, and will even slow the concentration needed to follow simple conversations.

Possible true effects

Marijuana increases the appetite and raises the heartbeat. Sensory distortions may occur. Speech may become incoherent because the drug affects the thought processes; this leads to time lags in conversation, which may just run out. The reduction of inhibitions may lead to behaviour foreign to the user in normal circumstances. The disinhibiting effects weaken cultural, religious, social and personal restraints. The extreme suggestibility leads to agreement to, or participation in, acts or sexual activities not normally indulged in without the influence of the drug.

This is especially so with young people; there is a high likelihood that they will become sexually active, and will risk all the attendant unwanted pregnancies and sexually transmitted diseases, including Aids.

Other true effects can include tremors; reduced body temperature; impairment of short-term memory and concentration, and of judgement and co-ordination. Users can find difficulty in sitting upright, in controlling the movement of their hands. They may find it hard to read, or to understand what they read, or to follow moving objects with their eyes. These effects may continue for hours after the consumption of cannabis. Users may feel quite confident that their reactions, co-ordination, and perceptions are quite normal while they are still under the drug; then they may drive a vehicle with lethal and tragic consequences to themselves and members of the public. Cannabis is also responsible for accidental deaths by drowning; for falls from heights, and for industrial accidents and fires. Many users become suspicious and aggressive; others may suffer attacks of panic and fear and confusion. During these attacks, they usually feel the need to flee to their homes, or to some other place of safety, and may be injured or killed during their flight.

Effects of an overdose

The active ingredients of cannabis are the 61 cannabinoids contained in hemp. These active ingredients, in combination, are known as THC (delta -9- tetrahydrocannibinol) which is dealt with below in detail. The actual strength of THC in cannabis has grown from about 0.5 per cent in the 1960s, to as much as 5 per cent and, in some cases, 11 per cent today. An overdose may cause the victim to suffer the unpleasant effects listed above. A victim should be taken for medical attention or supervision, especially as deep fatigue, paranoia, and psychosis are common.

Withdrawal symptoms

Although physical dependence is rated low, and psychological dependence only moderate, withdrawal may be very unpleasant, and the victim may suffer from insomnia, hyperactivity and loss of appetite.

HASHISH RESIN AND HASHISH OIL

Slang names: hash; hash oil

The leaves, seeds and other tissues of the hemp plant all contain the active cannabinoids desired by the user. When processed, the plant produces a concentrated resin and oil, an alcohol of cannabis; the seeds alone may contain 30 per cent of the oil.

Methods of use

Both the resin and the oil may be taken by mouth, but are more commonly smoked, usually in combination with tobacco. The implements used for smoking are an ordinary pipe; or a water pipe designed to concentrate the smoke.

Subjective effects

Because it is possible to concentrate the effects of the drug and so give stronger doses, all the effects of taking marijuana given above may be amplified; this includes the unpleasant effects, which usually last from 2 to 4hr.

Possible true effects

Again, all the true effects may be amplified sensations of the feelings given by taking marijuana. The concentration of the THC levels in hashish greatly increases the possibility of adverse reactions and their consequences.

Effects of an overdose

These are as for cannabis, but are even more likely to occur due to the concentration of cannabinoids in the resin and oil. Fatigue, paranoia and, very possibly, psychosis may result.

Withdrawal symptoms

The same as for marijuana; very unpleasant, but not necessarily life-threatening.

THC

Delta -9- tetrahydrocannabinol, abbreviated to THC for convenience, is not the name of a drug. It describes one of the 61 cannabinoids in hemp, which are the active ingredients, out of 400 or more different chemicals found in any cannabis preparation. THC may play an important role in current or future arguments over whether or not possession and use of cannabis should be legitimised in western democracies. It may even figure largely in the debate over the use of the description 'soft drug' which is loosely used to describe drugs other than narcotics (heroin, etc) stimulants (cocaine, etc), depressants (barbiturates, etc), and hallucinogens (LSD, etc).

The principal argument put forward by the pro-legalisation groups is primarily that cannabis does no more harm than tobacco and alcohol. That it is probably less harmful because, it is claimed, it has no long lasting effects, is not addictive, and can, therefore, be taken occasionally without risk. The groups quote any number of variations on this theme.

Many of these arguments began in the 1960s when 'pot'-smoking became almost obligatory for young people. At that time, the THC level in 'pot' was approximately 0.2 per cent, that is ⅕th of 1 part in 100 of a quantity of cannabis. By the 1970s, the level of THC in 'pot' rarely exceeded 0.5 per cent that is ½ of 1 part per 100. Currently, even in quite ordinary cannabis, the THC level has gone up to 5 per cent; that is 5 parts in 100. The levels in some expensive imported cannabis such as *sinsemilla* may be as high as 11 per cent; that is 11 parts per 100 of a quantity of cannabis.

For those who compare cannabis with alcohol, it may be of interest to note that this increase in potency, over the last 25 years, could only be equalled by an increase in the potency of a standard bottle of spirits (whisky or gin) of 55 times standard proof. This would increase the number of pub-measures obtained from a bottle, from 30 drinks to 1,650 drinks. The long term effects of cannabis, with these much raised levels of THC, cannot possibly be equated with the effects obtained from tests conducted upon those who used 'pot' in the 1960s and 1970s. Cannabis may have been, relatively, less harmful or addictive in those days, but it certainly does not qualify for the misleading, and potentially tragic, description of 'soft drug'. It has taken much effort, and very large scale medical and statistical studies, to indicate a link between the consumption of tobacco and certain types of cancer. The proponents of the legalisation of cannabis ignore the fact that they could be attempting to lay the foundation for a disaster in physical and mental health, to be played out in the not so distant future.

Long term effects of cannabis

The lungs Reduced lung capicity, shortness of breath, and chronic bronchitis are typical effects of smoking cannabis, especially, hashish. It also seems that the lungs' natural resistance to infection is much reduced. A direct link between lung cancer and cannabis smoking may not be absolutely provable because the evidence may be blurred by the fact that cannabis is frequently smoked in conjunction with tobacco; many cannabis smokers are also tobacco users. Tobacco and cannabis smoke are very similar, but cannabis smoke contains higher concentrations of cancer-causing carcinogens in its tars than are present in tobacco. Cannabis smokers habitually try to suck the smoke into their lungs as deeply as possible, in order to obtain the full effects of the drug; cigarette and pipe smokers normally inhale the smoke shallowly and, in most instances, though filters. It would seem that in addition to the various other adverse effects listed, any potential cannabis smoker would be well advised to consider very seriously the likelihood of contracting lung cancer.

The Heart Cannabis can raise the blood pressure and does increase the heart rate. This may not be too important if it happens infrequently, but unnecessary extra stress is never a good thing. It would be ill-advised for anyone suffering from chronic high blood pressure, hardening of the arteries, erratic heart rhythm, or any form of heart disease, to indulge in cannabis.

The Brain Changes have been observed in the brain's electrical activity that have been caused by the use of cannabis and that have continued after the use of the drug has ceased. It is not yet known whether or not these changes are harmful. The psychological dangers of cannabis are well documented; they include paranoia; delusions; hallucinations; and possible long-term psychosis. Flash-backs can occur some considerable time after drug use, and can be potentially life-endangering if, for example, the victim is driving a car, or walking across a busy road.

There is further potential danger in the fact that THC is fat-soluble and remains in the body for some considerable time after cannabis has been consumed. The THC is absorbed by the fatty tissues and stays in the fatty parts of the body cells. Even when released by the tissues, THC may be re-cycled through the body by means of re-absorpotion in the intestines. A quarter to a third may still remain in the user's body a week after smoking one marijuana cigarette. Traces of THC may remain in the body for much longer periods. In comparison, alcohol is water soluble and is easily washed out of the body, by natural processes within 24hr. It has been reported that in investigations into otherwise inexplicable aircraft crashes in the USA, quantities of THC were found in the bodies of the dead aircrew and may have been the cause of the crashes.

Evidence of genetic effects

Recent research has shown that male cannabis users have lower levels of the male hormone, testosterone, with reduced count and abnormal sperm. Exaggerated tremors, eyesight and reflex problems can be suffered by babies born of mothers who smoked cannabis during pregnancy.

19 Other Substances

SOLVENTS

Although any of the drugs of abuse may be obtained and used by people of all ages, the abuse of volatile solvents and of substances containing volatile solvents and aerosols is mainly a young person's activity. Volatile substances are liquids or salts that evaporate rapidly at ordinary temperature on exposure to the air. A solvent is a substance, generally a liquid, which is capable of dissolving other substances; or it may be a substance in which another substance is dissolved. And the aerosol, in this context, consists of substances in fine particles or droplets suspended in a gas under pressure in a container.

The vapour given off by these substances has an intoxicating effect when sniffed, or inhaled through the mouth. It is this intoxication which is sought by the users; and solvents can be bought legitimately almost anywhere.

Glues, model cements, rubber cement, cleaning fluid, paint thinners, petrol (gasoline), degreasers, typewriter correction fluid, adhesives, aerosol sprays, foam dispensers, cream dispensers, butane lighter gas, can all give a user the symptoms of drunkenness; but at a terrible risk. It must be pointed out that none of these substances is dangerous to the user when properly used in accordance with the instructions given on the containers in which they are supplied. Millions of people all over the world use them with no ill-effects.

Methods of use

The most commonly used solvents of abuse are contained in adhesives such as Evo-stick.

A quantity of the adhesive is put into a plastic bag and sniffed, or is inhaled through the mouth. Typewriter correction fluid may also be abused in this way. Aerosols may be used by spraying the contents into a container and inhaling by mouth or by sniffing it, or by inhaling straight from the aerosol container. Butane is easily obtained in a pressurised container and inhaled. Paint thinner, petrol, degreaser, and other easily vaporised liquids may be poured onto a cloth and inhaled from the cloth pressed to the face or wrapped around the head.

Subjective effective of abuse

Usual duration of effect from 4min to 2hr. The duration of effect varies widely with the substance abused. In the main, the effects are almost instantaneous, exaggerated feelings of physical comfort and wellbeing; buoyant feelings and sense of bodily health; excitement; a feeling of physical strength and power; a release of inhibitions.

Possible true effect

These substances are extremely dangerous and threaten any user with a whole variety of dreadful effects. Users lose co-ordination and experience visual distortion. Speech becomes slurred. They suffer loss of judgement. They become incapable of concentration and suffer memory loss. These effects can lead to accidents, including falls. They can smother to death, with their faces in the plastic bags used for sniffing and inhaling, or they may smother in the cloths soaked in solvent.

These substances make the user reckless; and violently aggressive by releasing inhibitions. Butane gas may cause suffocation if the pressurised spray penetrates the lungs; and the freezing action of the gas may damage the mouth and throat.

Other common effects are: serious eye, skin, and nose conditions; heart failure; nausea; stomach pains; muscle weakness; withering of muscle tissue; headaches; feeling of weakness; degeneration of the nervous system; damage to the liver and kidneys; jaundice; damage to the optic nerves and other nerves in the head; blindness, both temporary and permanent; destruction of bone marrow; some types of leukemia; anaemia; total kidney and liver failure. Almost any one of these effects, or any possible combination of them, can cause death, and the possibility of death from solvent and aerosol abuse is very high.

ALCOHOL

Alcoholic drinks consist chiefly of water and ethyl alcohol, 'ethanol'. They are manufactured by the process of fermentation which may use honey or fruits, vegetables or grains. The fermentation process yields a liquid that has an alcoholic content of 14 to 16 per cent, that is, 14 to 16 parts of alcohol to every hundred parts of water. The fermented liquid may be distilled to produce spirits which have a much higher alcohol content. Alcoholic drinks generally fall into four categories:

Beer, ale and lager, which usually contain 2 to 5 per cent alcohol, although there are 'special' beers and lagers manufactured, with an alcoholic content up to 6 per cent.

Wine, which usually has between 9 and 14 per cent alcohol.

The alcoholic content of 'fortified' wines such as sherry or port wine may be raised to as high as 20 per cent by the addition of brandy.

Distilled spirits, such as whisky, brandy, gin, rum or vodka usually have an alcoholic content of between 35 and 50 per cent. Some spirits may be specially processed to have an even higher alcohol content.

Subjective effects of alcohol – several hours

The subjective effects may be conditioned partly by the alcohol consumed, and partly by the surroundings in which the drinking is done. Generally the consumption of a small amount of alcohol (the first drink or two) gives the user a feeling of relaxation and reduction of anxiety; he may feel less tense socially than he would otherwise, due to the relaxation of inhibitions. As alcohol is absorbed into the bloodstream, the desired effects are felt quite rapidly – within 5 to 10min.

How much effect is felt from any given quantity of alcohol depends on a number of factors. How much alcohol is drunk and how strong it is; for example, approximately half a pint of beer or cider is equal to one measure of gin, which is equal to about one glass of wine. How much food there is in the drinker's stomach. How quickly he consumes the drink; what his body weight is; what kind of personality he has; and the surroundings in which the drink is consumed. Those who drink frequently develop a tolerance for alcohol; they may require more alcohol than a modest drinker to feel similar effects. An average drinker will begin to feel the effects of alcohol after about two pints of beer when he becomes less inhibited and more relaxed. A further two pints show up in slightly slurred and louder speech, and in the drinker becoming slightly clumsy. Gestures may be exaggerated and changes in general demeanour may become noticeable; for example, the shy man or timid girl may become the 'life and soul of the party'; jokes may seem funnier and sad events more tragic.

Possible true effects

Alcohol causes the blood vessels to dilate, which in turn may cause the rate of the drinker's heartbeat to vary; it may lower the blood pressure; cause the skin to flush; give a feeling of warmth; and increase loss of body heat. Quite small doses of alcohol can increase the rate of breathing, whilst greater amounts can slow the respiration down. Low concentrations of alcohol in beer and wines may act as an aid to digestion by increasing the production of stomach acid.

However, the higher concentrations of alcohol in spirits can irritate the lining of the stomach and can cause ill-effects, especially for people who suffer from stomach ulcers. Drinking alcohol increases the production of urine; going to the toilet can result in considerable loss of body fluids, despite the amount of liquid that has been consumed. This is noticeable in the dry mouth sensation the morning after the night before! The feeling of thirst may be felt for some hours, despite copious intake of fluids. It may encourage further consumption of alcohol on the principle of the 'hair of the dog that bit you'. Excessive consumption of alcohol can lead to acts of aggression and violence, crime, accident injuries and of acts of wanton destruction.

A combination of alcohol and motor vehicles can be lethal. After just a few drinks, a driver may feel perfectly in control of himself and his vehicle and yet be totally unable to deal with the simplest of co-ordinated acts. About one-third of all drivers, and up to a quarter of all adult pedestrians, killed in road accidents have blood alcohol levels above the legal limit. Death may also occur from the drinker choking on his own vomit whilst unconscious.

Effects of an overdose

A fine balance exists between the amount of alcohol that will put a drinker to sleep and the amount that may kill him. Even moderate consumption of alcohol, by someone unused to drinking, can result in death as a result of choking on vomit whilst unconscious. This becomes even more likely if the drinker takes a barbiturate or other depressant drug in combination with alcohol. Death can also result from depression of the respiratory system, and may also result from shock. A heavily unconscious user may also suffocate if face down on a soft pillow. It must be emphasised that it takes a very large quantity of alcohol to be consumed for any of these effects to occur, and that even the consumption of such a quantity rarely results in death.

Effects of withdrawal

Alcohol is to some people a drug of addiction, and withdrawal can be as severe and dangerous for them as withdrawal from any other drug of abuse. Common symptoms are agitation and anxiety; the 'shakes'; copious sweating; rapid, pounding heartbeat; rising temperature; nausea; vomiting.

For hardened alcoholics, the symptoms are even more severe, and withdrawal may be drawn out over a period of weeks. The sufferers may become disorientated, confused and delirious. They may experience psychosis caused by the poisons in their system; they may suffer from delusions and hallucinations; 'pink elephants' are no joke to someone drying out. Very high temperatures and extreme agitation can lead to convulsions. For those who are suffering from malnutrition as a result of their drinking habits, death may result from shock or failure of the respiratory system. For these people, expert medical help is essential.

Long term effects

The moderate use of alcohol – say, no more than 1 or 2 drinks per day – presents no serious health risk to any normally healthy person. It may even have a moderately beneficial effect. However, the consumption of between 5 and 7 pints of alcohol per day for a man, and 3½ to 5 pints for a woman, increases the chances of drinkers suffering serious physical and mental damage.

Heavy drinking of alcohol over a long period may lead to malnutrition as a result of the drinker being uninterested in food, or unwilling to use 'drinking money' to pay for food. Consequently, the drinker's resistance to infections becomes much lower, and his body's ability to function becomes much reduced. Heavy drinkers become deficient in essential B vitamins, which can result in severe damage to the nervous system and bring on mental disorders. Brain tissue can be destroyed, resulting in severe forgetfulness, the inability to concentrate, and the inability to make decisions.

The long term alcoholic may speak in slurred manner and walk with a drunken stagger even when sober, as a result of his reduced ability to control the muscles necessary for speech and walking. The liver and kidneys may suffer severe, damage. The liver can be scarred by inflammation, resulting in scar tissue that disrupts the liver's functions of removing body waste and producing substances essential to food digestion. The liver may be deformed by cirrhosis. If the liver damage becomes very severe, blood cannot pass through it, and internal bleeding may occur, resulting in death. Victims may also die from anaemia and failure of their blood to clot.

Alcoholics tend to be overweight, and they may develop diabetes, they may suffer from swollen glands, have swollen and bleeding gums and they may become more vulnerable to infections. Some male victims become impotent. Heart attacks and cancer are particularly common, including cancer of the liver.

Women who drink heavily risk: liver disease; ulcers; heart attacks; disorders of the blood circulation; brain damage. Death may result from cirrhosis of the liver; accidents; heart damage; and suicide. Women who drink during pregnancy risk birth defects in their babies. The babies may be retarded, they may have heart abnormalities or abnormalities of the lungs or the sexual organs. They may suffer facial disfigurement and joint defects. Most of these defects, known as foetal alcohol syndrome, seem to be caused during the first three months of pregnancy.

TOBACCO

It is the name given to the plant, and to cured leaves of several species of the plant *Nicotiana*. The name tobacco is derived from the American Indian name for the rolled cylinder of leaf prepared for smoking and for the tube used to inhale smoke. Tobacco was introduced to England in 1565.

Methods of use

Most tobacco is sold in the form of cigarettes. The remainder is commonly sold as cigars, as pipe tobacco and snuff. Some is sold for chewing. Recently, packaged wads of chewing tobacco have been put on the market aimed at young people; an effort is being made to ban the sale of this product.

Among the other chemicals in tobacco are nicotine and related alkaloids, which give the narcotic and habit-forming effects that account for the popularity of smoking around the world. Because the smoke is inhaled into the lungs, the active ingredients enter the bloodstream and quickly reach the brain. Nicotine is a stimulant and smokers, to some degree, use the stimulant effect to lessen fatigue and tolerate monotonous tasks.

Subjective effects

Relieves stress and anxiety. The stimulating or relaxing effect declines rapidly, encouraging further smoking.

True effects

Long term smoking is clearly indicated as conbtributory factor in heart disease, in the formation of blood clots, in heart attacks, lung infections, in strokes, bad blood circulation, bronchitis, and in cancer of the mouth and ulcers. Heavy smoking materially reduces life expectancy. Women who smoke during pregnancy tend to have smaller babies, and to run the risk of losing the baby before or soon after birth.

Withdrawal

Regular smokers deprived of tobacco tend to become restless, irritable, and depressed. There is a strong degree of dependence on the tobacco.

20 Multiple Abuse (Polyabuse)

Addicts frequently combine two or more drugs in an attempt to reduce unpleasant symptoms experienced in drug taking. One method is known as speedballing where a combination of injections of cocaine and heroin are taken intravenously. It is claimed that this decreases the tenseness, irritability, and overactivity associated with cocaine. Addicts may also use heroin after a cocaine 'high' to help them to 'come down' more easily.

Other drugs may be used which have the effect of depressing the central nervous system, the most common being methaqualone, barbiturates, benzodiazepines, and alcohol. The addicts may become physically dependent on these depressants in addition to their cocaine addiction. Any multiple abuse of drugs is extremely dangerous and can be life-threatening.

Useful Addresses

Department of Education and Science
Publication Despatch Centre, Honeypot Lane, Stanmore, Middlesex, HA7 1AZ
Copies of *Drug Misuse and the Young* and of other DES publications are available from this address.

Department of Health and Social Security
Dept DM, DHSS Leaflet Unit, PO Box 21, Stanmore, Middlesex, HA7 1AY
DHSS has produced three brief publications which are available from the above address:
Drug Misuse: A Basic Briefing
Drugs: What Parents Can Do
What Every Parent Should Know About Drugs

Families Anonymous
88 Caledonian Road, London, N1 9DN

Home Office
E5 Division (Drugs Branch), Queen Anne's Gate, London, SW1H 9AT
Tackling Drug Misuse: A Summary Of The Government's Strategy was published by the Home Office in March 1985.

Health Education Council (HEC)
Education and Training Division, 78 New Oxford Street, London, WC1A 1AH
The HEC's activities are directed mainly towards general health and social education. It has supported projects on development of curriculum and materials for health and social education in schools

and many of these projects touch on legal and illegal drugs. Resource lists on drug, alcohol and smoking education are available free from HEC's library. HEC supports Health Education Officers in the field and also supports the training work of TACADE and other agencies.

Health Education Council
12-19 Project, Health Education Unit, Department of Education, Southampton University, Southampton, SO9 5NH
The project includes the Schools Council/Health Education Council 13–18 project. It is concerned with curriculum development co-ordination and in-service work in the broad field of health/personal/social education.
Publications include:
Developing Health Education – A Co-ordinator's Guide (Forbes Publications Ltd)
Health Education 13–18 (Forbes Publications Ltd)
Alcohol, Drugs and Smoking – an annotated resource list available free from the Project, HEC or local health education sources.

The project is currently developing additional material and strategies for the 16 plus age group intended for educational and youth work settings.

HMSO
49 High Holborn, London, WC1V 6HB
A number of official publications on drug abuse are available from HMSO bookshops or through booksellers.

Institute for the Study of Drug Dependence (ISDD)
1-4 Hatton Place, Hatton Gardens, London, EC1N 8ND
ISDD maintains a comprehensive reference library on non-medical use of drugs, and produces information leaflets, health and social education materials and materials for training of professionals. Information on specific topics can be obtained through ISDD's library and information service.
Publication include:
Facts and Feelings about Drugs but Decisions about Situations (a drug education course for use in secondary schools)
Health Career (a project based course of health and social education

in which drug, alcohol and solvent misuse are related to work, culture and leisure); and a multi-disciplinary in-service training pack for local courses.

Each of these manuals costs £4.50 plus 15% postage.

Lifeline
Regional Drug Training Unit, Prestwich Hospital, Prestwich, Lancashire

Narcotics Anonymous
Drug Abuse, PO Box 246, London, SW10
Narcotics Anonymous is a self-help organisation for misusers. It has a number of local groups.

National Association of Boys Clubs
24 Highbury Grove, London, N5 2EA

National Association of Young People's Counselling and Advisory Service
17-23 Albany Street, Leicester, LE1 6CD
NAYPCAS aims to promote and develop youth counselling and advisory work. It issues a newsletter and quarterly bulletins for members; and provides training in counselling.

National Association of Youth Clubs
Keswick House, 30 Peacock Lane, Leicester, LE1 5NY

National Council for Voluntary Youth Services
26 Albion Street, Leicester, LE1 6GD

National Intermediate Treatment Federation (NITF)
c/o Save The Children Fund, Goldhawk House, 49 Goldhawk Road, London, W12 8QP

National Youth Bureau
Albion Street, Leicester, LE1 6GD
NYB stimulates innovation in youth work and social education; it publishes *Youth and Society*; it supports regional and local training initiatives for youth workers and publishers material such as the

youth workers' pack, *Enfranchisement*, which includes information on the legal aspects of alcohol and drugs.

St John Ambulance Association
Edwina Mountbatten House, 63 York Street, London, W1H 1PS
Their publication, *Emergency Aid in Schools* (price £1.95), includes a comprehensive chapter on 'Poisons, Drug and Alcohol Abuse, Glue Sniffing, Foreign Bodies'. It is available from St. John Ambulance Supplies Department, Priory House, St. John's Lane, London, EC1M 4DA.

SCODA Standing Conference on Drug Abuse
1-4 Hatton Place, Hatton Gardens, London, EC1N 8ND
SCODA has a full list of services throughout the country. SCODA publications include a six-weekly newsletter (£10 annually), guides to specialist non-statutory services and a series of fieldwork surveys on drug misuse.

South Wales Association for the Prevention of Drug Addiction
111 Cowbridge Road East, Canton, Cardiff, CF1 9AG
SWAPA provides a 24 hour call-in service for people with drug problems; available to give advice and monitor progress.

Teachers Advisory Council on Alcohol and Drug Education (TACADE)
2 Mount Street, Manchester, M2 SN9
TACADE provides education and training material primarily related to formal education system. Publications include a basic information leaflet, *Drugs Basic Facts* (10p), basic teaching material, *Drugs Teacher Pack* (£3.60), and a fuller education course in the misuse of drugs and other substances, *Free to Choose* (£19.95). A termly school publication, *Minotors*, is issued. A list of material is available.

Welsh Office
Information Division, Cathays Park, Cardiff, CF1 3NQ
Publications issued by DHSS on drugs, also this booklet, are available in English and Welsh from the Welsh Office.

Young Men's Christian Association
National Council of YMCAs, 640 Forest Road, London, E17 3DZ
YMCA has 200 local centres throughout the country. An investigation into drug and solvent misuse has led to a development programme and new resources, including a video

Youth Forum on Alcohol and Substance Abuse
West 1 Ward, Whitchurch Hospital, Cardiff, CF4 7XB
The forum is a working party of teachers, youth workers, health educators doctors and students. Its aim is to consult young people about community problems relating to drugs and alcohol in order to increase awareness of the problems; to receive opinion and advice and to provide conditions for decisions to be made on prevention of abuse. It arranges international youth conferences on alcohol and drug abuse.

ORGANISATIONS FOR THOSE IN TROUBLE IN BRITAIN

National 24-hours Emergency Telephone Service: **Release** *Tel*: (01) 6038654.
Advice and information on legal and drug-related problems.

Narcotics Anonymous
PO Box 246, c/o 47 Milman Street, London, SW10. *Tel*: (01) 3516794 and 3516066 (24-hour answerphone service)
Self-help group for drug dependents. Meeting and contacts in various parts of the country. Office usually staffed 2.30pm–8pm daily.

Alcoholics Anonymous
PO Box 514, 11 Redcliffe Gardens, London, SW10. *Tel*: (01) 3529779
This is the address of the main Alcoholics Anonymous centre, which can provide local contact addresses (your local telephone directory also may have listings).

TRANX
17 Peel Road, Wealdstone, Harrow, Middlesex, HA3 7QX. *Tel*: (01) 427 2065

Self-help group for people with tranquillizer problems. It provides contacts in other parts of the country.

Families Anonymous
88 Caledonian Road, London, N1 9DN. *Tel*: (01) 278 8805 (24-hour answerphone)
Advice and support group for families and friends of drug users. Meetings and contacts throughout the country. Hours: Mon–Fri., 1pm–4pm.

Al-Anon
61 Dover Street, London, SE1 4YF. *Tel*: (01) 403 0888
Al-Anon is associated with Alcoholics Anonymous and provides group support for the relatives and friends of alcoholics. Addresses of local groups are available from the address above.

Lifeline Project Day Centre
Jodrell Street, Manchester, M3 3HE. *Tel*: (061) 832 6353
Day centre offering support and practical help to drug users, their families and friends; assistance with legal problems; assessment and referral for rehabilitation; advice and information to professionals. Also training and educational facilities for professionals and organizations. Parents' groups attached. Hours: Mon–Fri, 10am–6pm.

SCODA
Ainslie House, 11 St. Colme Street, Edinburgh. *Tel*: (031) 226 2293

Andrew Duncan Clinic
Royal Edinburgh Hospital, Morningside Place, Edinburgh, EH10. *Tel*: (031) 447 2011

Residential/Rehabilitation Simpson House Drugs Project
52 Queen Street, Edinburgh, *Tel*: (031) 225 1054
Referral, day centre, counselling, health advice, family support.

Information & Resource Unit on Addiction
82 West Regent Street, Glasgow, G2. *Tel*: (041) 332 0062

Strathclyde Social Work Department
Strathclyde House, 4 India Street, Glasgow, G2. *Tel*: (041) 227 2301

Aberdeen Community Drugs Advice & Counselling Service
(No premises at present). *Tel*: (0224 646491)

Craig Dunain Hospital
Inverness IV3. *Tel*: (0463) 234101

Assistance on Addiction
c/o Planning Department, 17 Blackfaulds Place, Fauldhouse, West Lothian. *Tel*: (0501) 70206

Royal Dundee Hospital
Dundee, DD2. *Tel*: (0328) 580441.

North Wales Association for the Prevention of Addiction
19 Lombard Street, Porthmadoc, LL49 9AP
Information advice and support for local drug takers.

South Wales APA
11 Cowbridge Road East, Cardiff, CF1 9AC. *Tel*: (0222) 26113
SWAPA provides 24-hour nationwide counselling service. Publications sent out (with sae) Local education/talks.

Shaftesbury Square Hospital
116-118 Great Victoria Street, Belfast, BT2 7BG. *Tel*: (0232) 229 808

City Roads (Crisis Intervention) Ltd
356/358 City Road, London, EC1
Tel: (01) 278 8671
Short-stay detoxification for multiple drug users in crisis. Will take couples. Cannot accommodate children. Catchment area: Greater London.

UNITED STATES DRUG ABUSE PREVENTION AND TREATMENT COORDINATORS

Alabama Commissioner, Department of Mental Health, 200 Interstate Park Drive, P.O. Box 3710, Montgomery, Alabama 36193/(205) 271 9209

Alaska Coordinator, Office of Alcoholism & Drug Abuse, Department of Health & Social Services, Pouch H 05 F, Juneau, Alaska 99811/(907) 586 6201

Arizona Manager, Drug Abuse Section, Department of Health Services, Division of Behavioral Health Services, 2500 East Van Buren, Phoenix, Arizona 85008/(602) 255 1240

Arkansas Director, Office on Alcohol and Drug Abuse Prevention, 1515 West Seventh Avenue, Suite 300, Little Rock, Arkansas 72202/(501) 371 2603

California Director, Department of Alcohol and Drug Abuse, 111 Capitol Mall, Sacramento, California 95814/(916) 445 1940

Colorado Director, Alcohol and Drug Abuse Division, Department of Health, 4210 East 11th Avenue, Denver, Colorado 80220/(303) 320 6137

Connecticut Executive Director, Connecticut Alcohol and Drug Abuse Commission, 999 Asylum Avenue, Third Floor, Hartford, Connecticut 06105/(203) 566 4145

Delaware Chief, Bureau of Alcoholism and Drug Abuse, 1901 North DuPont Highway, Newcastle, Delaware 19720/(302) 421 6101

District of Columbia Chief, Health Planning and Development, 1875 Connecticut Avenue, N.W., Suite 836, Washington, D.C. 20009/(202) 673 7481

Florida Director, Drug Abuse Program, 1317 Winewood Boulevard, Building 6, Room 163A, Tallahassee, Florida 32301/(904) 488 0900

Georgia Director, Alcohol and Drug Section, Division of Mental Health, Mental Retardation and Substance Abuse, Department of Human Resources, 47 Trinity Avenue, S.W. Atlanta, Georgia 30334/(404) 656 4918

Hawaii Branch Chief, Alcohol and Drug Abuse Branch, Department of Health, P.O. Box 3378, Honolulu, Hawaii 96801/(808) 548 4280

Idaho Director, Bureau of Substance Abuse, Department of Health and Welfare, 450 West State Street, Boise, Idaho 83720/(208) 334 4368

Illinois Director, Illinois Dangerous Drugs Commission, 300 North State Street, Suite 1500, Chicago, Illinois 60610/(312) 822 9860

Indiana Director, Division of Addiction Services, Department of Mental Health, 429 North Pennsylvania Street, Indianapolis, Indiana 46204/(317) 232 7816

Iowa Director, Iowa Department of Substance Abuse, 505 Fifth Avenue, Insurance Exchange Building, Suite 202, Des Moines, Iowa 50319/(515) 281 3641

Kansas Commissioner, Alcohol and Drug Abuse Services, 2700 West Sixth Street, Biddle Building, Topeka, Kansas 66606/(913) 296 3925

Kentucky Manager, Alcohol and Drug Branch, Bureau for Health Services, Department of Human Services, Department of Human Resources, 275 East Main Street, Frankfort, Kentucky 40621/(502) 564 2880

Louisiana Director, Office of Mental Health and Substance Abuse, 655 North Fifth Street, P.O. Box 4049, Baton Rouge, Louisiana 70821/(504) 342 2565

Maine Director, Office of Alcoholism and Drug Abuse Prevention, Bureau of Rehabilitation, 32 Winthrop Street, Augusta, Maine 04330/(207) 289 2781

Maryland Director, Maryland State Drug Abuse Administration, 201 West Preston Street, Baltimore, Maryland 21201/(301) 383 3312

Massachusetts Director, Division of Drug Rehabilitation, 600 Washington Street, Boston, Massachusetts 02111/(617) 727 8617

Michigan Director, Office of Substance Abuse Services, Department of Public Health, 3500 North Logan Street, Lansing, Michigan 48909/(517) 373 0967

Minnesota Director, Chemical Dependency Program Division, Department of Public Welfare, 4th Floor Centennial Building, 658 Cedar, St. Paul, Minnesota 55155/(612) 296 4610

Mississippi Director, Division of Alcohol and Drug Abuse, Department of Mental Health, 11th Floor, Robert E. Lee Office Building, Jackson, Mississippi 39201/(601) 359 1297

Missouri Director, Division of Alcoholism and Drug abuse, Department of Mental Health, 2002 Missouri Boulevard, P.O. Box 687, Jefferson City, Missouri 65101/(314) 751 4942

Montana Administrator, Alcohol and Drug Abuse Division, Department of Institutions, Helena, Montana 59601/(406) 449 2827

Nebraska Director, Division on Alcoholism and Drug Abuse, Department of Public Institutions, P.O. Box 94728, Lincoln, Nebraska 68509/(402) 471 2851

Nevada Chief, Bureau of Alcohol and Drug Abuse, Department of Human Resources, 505 East King Street, Carson City, Nevada 89710/(702) 885 4790

New Hampshire Director, Office of Alcohol and Drug Abuse Prevention, Health and Welfare Building, Hazen Drive, Concord, New Hampshire 03301/(603) 271 4627

New Jersey Director, Division of Narcotic and Drug Abuse Control, 129 East Hanover Street, Trenton, New Jersey 08625/(609) 292 5760

New Mexico Chief, Drug Abuse Bureau, Behavioral Health Services Division, P.O. Box 968, Santa Fe, New Mexico 87504/(505) 984 0020

New York Assistant Director, Division of Substance Abuse Services, Executive Park South, Box 8200, Albany, New York 12203/(518) 457 7629

North Carolina Deputy Director, Alcohol and Drug Abuse Section, Division of Mental Health and Mental Retardation Services, 325 North Salisbury Street, Raleigh, North Carolina 27611/(919) 733 4670

North Dakota Director, Division of Alcoholism and Drug Abuse, Department of Human Services, State Capitol, Bismarck, North Dakota 58505/(701) 224 2767

Ohio Chief, Bureau of Drug Abuse, 65 South Front Street, Columbus, Ohio 43215/(614) 466 9023

Oklahoma Director, Alcohol and Drug Programs, Department of Mental Health, P.O Box 53277, Capitol Station, 4545 North Lincoln Boulevard, Suite 100 E. Terrace, Oklahoma City, Oklahoma 73152/(405) 521 0044

Oregon Associate Administrator, Mental Health Divison, 2575 Bittern Street, N.E., Salem, Oregon 97310/(503) 378 2163

Pennsylvania Deputy Secretary, Drug and Alcohol Programs, Department of Health, P.O. Box 90, Harrisburg, Pennsylvania 17108/(717) 787 9857

Rhode Island Assistant Director, Department of Mental Health, Mental Retardation and Hospitals, Division of Substance Abuse, Substance Abuse, Administration Building, Cranston, Rhode Island 02920/(401) 464 2091

South Carolina Director, South Carolina Commission on Alcohol and Drug Abuse, 3700 Forest Drive, Columbia, South Carolina 29204/(803) 758 2521

South Dakota Director, Division of Alcohol and Drug Abuse, Joe Foss Building, Pierre, South Dakota 57501/(605) 773 4806

Tennessee Assistant Commissioner, Alcohol and Drug Abuse Services, Department of Mental Health and Mental Retardation, James K. Polk Building, 505 Deaderick Street, Nashville, Tennessee 37219/(615) 741 1921

Texas Director, Drug Abuse Prevention Division, Department of Community Affairs, 2015 South IH 35, Austin, Texas 78741/(512) 443 4100

Utah Director, Division of Alcoholism and Drugs, 150 West North Temple, Suite 350, P.O. Box 2500, Salt Lake City, Utah 84110/(801) 533 6532

Vermont Director, Alcohol and Drug Abuse Division, 103 South Main Street, Waterbury, Vermont 05676/(802) 241 2170

Virginia Assistant Commissioner, Division of Substance Abuse, Department of Mental Health and Mental Retardation, 109 Governor Street, P.O. Box 1797, Richmond, Virginia 23214/(804) 786 5313

Washington Director, Bureau of Alcoholism and Substance Abuse, Department of Social and Health Services, Mail Stop OB44W, Olympia, Washington 98504/(206) 753 5866

West Virginia Director, Division of Alcohol and Drug Abuse, State Capitol, 1800 Kanawaha Boulevard East, Charleston, West Virginia 25305/(304) 348 2276

Wisconsin Director, Bureau of Alcohol and Other Drug Abuse, 1 West Wilson Street, P.O. Box 7851, Madison, Wisconsin 53707/(608) 266 2717

Wyoming Director, Alcohol and Drug Abuse Programs, Hathaway Building, Cheyenne, Wyoming 82002/(307) 777 7115

DEA Divison Offices

Atlanta Field Division Richard B. Russell Federal Building, 75 Spring St. S.W., Room 740, Atlanta, Georgia 30303/404/221 4401

Boston Field Division G-64 JFK Federal Building, Boston, Massachusetts 02203/617/223 2170

Chicago Field Division 500 Dirksen Federal Building, 219 S. Dearborn Street, Chicago, Illinois 60604/312/353 7875

Dallas Field Division 1880 Regal Row, Dallas, Texas 75235/214/767 7151

Denver Field Division 316 U.S. Customs House, 721 19th Street, Denver, Colorado 80201/303/844 3951

Detroit Field Division 357 Federal Building, 231 W. Lafayette, Detroit, Michigan 48226/313/226 7290

Houston Field Division 333 West Loop North, Suite 300, Houston, Texas 77024/713/229 2950

Los Angeles Field Division Suite 800, 350 S. Figueroa St., Los Angeles, California 90071/213/688 2650

Miami Field Division 8400 N.W. 53rd Street, Miami, Florida 33166/305/591 4870

Newark Field Division 970 Broad Street, 806 Federal Office Building, Newark, New Jersey 07102/201/645 6060

New Orleans Field Division 1661 Canal Street, Suite 2200, New Orleans, Louisiana 70112/504/589 3894

New York Field Division 555 W. 57th Street, Suite 1900, New York, New York 10019/212/399 5151

Philadelphia Field Division 10224 William J. Green Federal Building, 600 Arch Street, Philadelphia, Pennsylvania 19106/215/597 9530

Phoenix Field Division 1980 Valley Bank Center, 201 N. Central, Phoenix, Arizona 85073/602/261 4866

San Diego Field Division 402 W. 35th Street, National City, California 92050/619/585 9600

San Francisco Field Division Room 12215, 450 Golden Gate Avenue, San Francisco, California 94102/415/556 6771

Seattle Field Division Suite 301, 220 W. Mercer, Seattle, Washington 98119/206/442 5443

St. Louis Field Division 200 Chromallory Plaza, 120 S. Central Avenue, St. Louis, Missouri 63105/314/425 3241

Washington Field Division Room 2558, 400 Sixth St., S.W., Washington, D.C. 20024/202/724 7834

Afterword

Having read this far you will have almost certainly come to the conclusion that drug addiction is a threat to the whole of the population of this planet, and especially to young people. A threat created by evil and greedy men and their corrupt helpers. You will also have noted that at least one country, China, has cleared this great evil from their land despite its deep and traditional roots. Whether or not you approve of the methods employed by the Chinese, they have proved that drug addiction and the drug traffic can be eradicated despite the claims by some western apologists for the drug traders that drug addiction is a social condition which can only be modified and not cured. A question frequently asked at drug lectures and seminars is 'What can I as an individual do about the drug traffic?' Here are some suggestions.

It is vital to start an organisation of concerned people in order to put pressure on politicians, bureaucrats, and even the police, to take action on drugs locally, nationally, and internationally. Form a local branch of, say, Parents Against Drug Abuse, and use it to educate your neighbours and children by distributing information on drug abuse through community organisations, schools, youth groups, Women's Institutes, clubs etc. Keep pressuring your local political representative, local councillors and police to ensure that they know you want action on drugs.

Do not accept excuses for inaction from anyone in authority: *your* kids and *your* society are at stake. A favourite stalling device by the authorities is the claim that precipitate action could upset delicate trade or diplomatic initiatives with some foreign state . . . but remember that all the trade and all the diplomacy in the world can not help them once they are hooked on heroin! And as a tax payer, you are the one who pays the salaries of these individuals in high places. They should not treat your natural concern arrogantly or negligently; demand action and see that you get it.

There are some very active and useful organisations in the United States of America from whom advice and encouragement may be obtained. They have had to fight to become established and listened to and their experience could be of great help to you. Some useful addresses:

Families In Action (FIA)
Suite 300, 3845 N. Druid Hills Road, Decatur, Georgia, USA, 30033.

Families in Action is a community-based parents' group. It collects and distributes information about drugs and youth and does research on the effects of drugs.

National Federation of Parents for a Drug Free Youth (NFP)
1820 Franwell Avenue, Suite 16, Silver Spring, Maryland 20902, USA.

NFP consists of more than 8,000 self-help parent groups in the USA that have banded together to deal with the problem of drug abuse among children. Publications, resource materials and brochures can be purchased.

Parents' Resource Institute for Drug Education (PRIDE)
University Plaza, Georgia State University, Atlanta, Georgia, 30303, USA.

PRIDE is a non-profit organisation which provides current research information on drug abuse. It also helps concerned citizens organise parent groups, parent-school teams and community action groups. Its publications include books, pamphlets and a quarterly newsletter. PRIDE also offers films and audio and visual cassettes for sale and rent. Please remember that the organisations listed above are voluntary, self-funded organisations. If you wish to write to them please enclose International Postal Reply coupons. Postage is expensive! A word of warning – do not let political interest groups or activists take over your anti-drugs group. You are out to influence people of all political persuasions in the interests of your children and your society, you are also aiming at educating children of parents of all races, creeds, colours and political views . . . you can not afford to be partisan about anything other than defeating the drug traffickers.

It is as well to end this book with a reminder that the majority of young people do *not* take drugs not even alcohol or tobacco. However, if you suspect that a member of your family might be taking drugs then consider following this plan of action.

Stay calm! It could be that what you think is evidence of possible drug abuse might only be evidence that your youngster has achieved the dreadful stage of adolescence that all parents have to survive! Breathe deeply and try to remember your own adolescence. Sit down with a cup of tea or coffee and go back to the 'Answers to Basic Questions' near the beginning of the book. If you are still convinced that your youngster may be taking drugs then seek professional help. If you do not have a skilled priest or family doctor you can turn to, get out your telephone book, or go to your local library and find the address of any of the organisations who are skilled in dealing with these problems.

Whatever you do, do not despair and do not feel personally guilty. Parents are faced with immense external influences being exercised over their children . . . it is quite surprising how many of the youngsters turn out very well despite this. Good luck to you.

Acknowledgements

This book would have been impossible without the encouragement and assistance of many people and organisations. Some of the people who helped me must remain anonymous for their own protection, but they know who they are and I am most grateful to them. Some of the calculations and other facts about the drug traffic in Britain could not have been obtained without the invaluable assistance of 'Worzel' an ex-drugs squad person, to whom I must address my great appreciation. I am particularly indebted to Mr Peter Davis and his staff in the Directorate General for Information and Public Relations in the European Parliament, Luxembourg, for their energetic assistance which supplied me with vital and up to date factual information.

Because of the difficulty of obtaining unbiased information about drugs the major world source is the splendid US Drug Enforcement Agency in Washington DC, USA. I thank them and their efficient and helpful staff in the American Embassy in London.

Thanks to Mrs Pauline Cole of Hen Fwthyn, in Dyfed who worked long and hard at deciphering my writing and typing my manuscript.

I must acknowledge that this book might not have been started without the active encouragement of the splendid ladies of the Dyfed Federation of Women's Institutes. These ladies are formidable allies and great supporters and I thank them all.

Mr D. Sweeney, Department of Health, Woden, ACT, Australia.

Dept. Of Health, Wellington, New Zealand.

'Kiwi Grogger', Wellington, New Zealand.

Dr J. O'Connor, Drug Advisory and Treatment Centre, Jervis Street Hospital, Dublin 1, Ireland.

'Baltic Ivan', Hamburg, Germany.

Mr C. McEnenery, Statistics Section, Drugs Squad, Garda, Harcourt Square, Harcourt St., Dublin 2, Ireland.

'Lapin', Toronto, Canada.

Lastly, my thanks to my wife Barbara, chief advisor and critic!